Simon Benson:

Immigrant, Lumberman, Philanthropist

A Biography by

Chester G. Benson

Copyright © 2024 Chester G. Benson All rights reserved

No part of this book may be reproduced, or stored in a retrieval system,
or transmitted in any form or by any means, electronic, mechanical,
photocopying, recording, or otherwise,
without express written permission of the publisher.

ISBN-13: 979-8-9909253-1-1

Printed in the United States of America

To Darcy, for her endless love, support, and encouragement

And to Chris: I'm sorry you never got to read this

No one has the right to die and not leave something to the public and for the public good.

-- Simon Benson

Table of Contents

Introduction……………………………………………1

Author's Note…………………………………...……6

Chapter 1: Early Years.…………………………....9

Chapter 2: Times of Trial and Tragedy..………………34

Chapter 3: Innovation and Success…………………72

Chapter 4: Crowning Enterprise: The Rafts………...119

Chapter 5: New Perspectives, New Interests………...162

Chapter 6: The Columbia River Highway…………...201

Chapter 7: Final Contributions, Final Honors, and "Retirement"..................................254

Afterword..282

Bibliography..294

SIMON BENSON

Introduction

Simon Benson's life seems like a template of the immigrant's vision of the American Dream. He was born in 1851 into a poor farming family in central Norway. As a teenager he came to America with his family. He and likely his parents and siblings as well only received a few years of formal education at most, focusing instead on working to help support their family in both countries. He worked as a farmhand at first, then as a logger and in lumber mills in Wisconsin in his late teens and early twenties. After he married, he opened a small general store. But the store soon burned down so with his wife and toddler son he decided to seek greener pastures in the Pacific Northwest. Literally within a few days of his arrival in Portland, Oregon, he had found work as a logger again, for much better pay than he had earned previously, and a few months after that he had accumulated enough money to start his own logging operation. He experienced some successes and some failures, and then at a time of crisis in his life he came to a major turning point. His wife died, which led to serious soul-searching and a crucial decision: Benson no longer felt

SIMON BENSON

willing to go through life as a minor, mediocre business owner. Instead, he would bet everything to become a significant figure in the logging industry. He gambled on embracing new technology in order to rise above his peers in the industry. The bet paid off. Benson's innovative practices and new inventions led to great financial success and increasingly large and ambitious operations. From this point on, he suffered no more serious setbacks. By the time he retired around 1910 he had amassed a considerable personal fortune. He had proved to himself and the world beyond any doubt that he was an outstanding businessman, an expert at all aspects of the logging and lumber industry, and, as we shall see, an informally trained but highly competent engineer.

In the following decade after he sold his logging and lumber company, he added something else to his list of qualities and accomplishments: he showed that he was a dedicated philanthropist with an extraordinary vision of the future for Oregon in general and Portland in particular. He embarked on a series of projects that would make him a household name throughout the region. Rightly believing that cars and tourism would play a significant role in Oregon's future, he helped to spearhead and underwrite major highway projects, notably what is now called the

SIMON BENSON

Historic Columbia River Highway, a scenic route through the spectacular Columbia River Gorge east of Portland. Many commercials for cars are filmed there; it is likely nearly everyone in the country has seen glimpses of the highway's immense beauty, though they may not realize it. As part of his work with the highway he bought and donated the land around Multnomah Falls, one of Oregon's scenic highlights. Along with this project, Benson also donated money for construction of a public polytechnic high school in Portland. He gave more than twenty beautiful, ornate drinking fountains to the city as well. And along the way, Benson showed that he also had talent in running an entirely different kind of business: he built and successfully ran two hotels.

Eventually, in his seventies, Benson retired to the warmth of Southern California. Even there he enjoyed keeping his hand in with investments and advised others as well, including some celebrities. He died in Los Angeles in 1942, a few weeks short of his ninety-first birthday.

Simon Benson's legacy lives on in Oregon. The high school that bears his name remains one of the leading public schools in Portland. Though he sold it more than a century ago, the Benson Hotel still bears his name and still stands as one of Portland's finest lodgings as well. The Benson Bubbler fountains are still beloved by locals and tourists. Multnomah Falls is one of the state's most visited scenic spots, with more than two million visitors from all over the world each year; the distinctive pedestrian bridge across the falls still bears his name and just down the road is the Benson State Recreation Area, which includes Benson Lake. Benson's Portland house, which stood empty and decaying for many years, has been beautifully restored and moved to the campus of Portland State University, which also has named its annual fund-raising dinner for him.

Yet while it is difficult to avoid hearing the name Benson in Portland, few people nowadays have any idea who Simon Benson was and what he did. Just a few years after he retired to California he had already been forgotten in Oregon. The former "first citizen" came up for a visit and a headline writer identified him only as a "former Oregonian." A member of the staff of the Oregon Historical Society whom I spoke with had never heard of him, and neither had some people I met who worked at the World Forestry Center in Portland. Portland State University proudly uses his name and his house, but it pays little attention to the man himself. His entrepreneurial success, his innovation, his embracing and development of new technology could make him a strong role model for a modern urban university, but Portland State has ignored this. It makes one wonder why the school bought and restored his house, which now serves as office space for its alumni association.

His legacy remains, and his name is still widely heard around Portland, but the man himself has largely been forgotten by Oregonians. This book is for them. The man himself, and not just his name, deserves to be remembered.

SIMON BENSON

Author's Note

The first challenge facing someone who wants to write a biography of Simon Benson is learning the original name with which he was born. He and his brothers adopted the name Benson when they came to America because they thought it sounded more "American." He also Anglicized the spelling of his first name. Originally, his first name was "Simen," and his last name was a patronymic: he was Simen Bergersen, the son of Berger. His father Berger likewise had as his last name Iversen, for he was the son of Iver. His mother was Karen Stenersdatter, the daughter of Stener. People throughout Scandinavia had used patronymics for centuries; Icelanders still use them instead of consistent family surnames to this day. In Norway, regular surnames only became a legal requirement in 1925. This use of patronymics has led to considerable confusion among people trying to write about Simon Benson's early years. A number of writers get it wrong, including the author of Benson's profile in the *Oregon History Project*, who misspells his first name as Simon and calls him "Simon Berger Iversen." Portland State University, which bought and renovated his house and named its fundraising dinner after him, also refers to Benson as "Simon Iversen," while still another writer misspells both names and calls him "Simon Bergerson." Another writer, one of his own descendants, says his name was "Simon Berger-Iverson," hyphenating his father's name and patronymic. Fred Lockley, author of *History of the Columbia River Valley, from the Dalles to the Sea*, calls Simon's father "Berger Bergersen," which at least allows him to identify Benson's original surname correctly.

For many generations, some Norwegians would also affix a "farm name" to their own names. This would identify them with the major farm in the region, perhaps even the land on which they were tenant farmers. In the part of Norway where Benson grew up, this was the Klaeve farm, and some writers today attach "Klave," or a variant spelling, to Simen Bergersen's and his family members' names. However, the use of such names was not universal, and there is no clear evidence that this particular family ever used it. They appear as Bergersen, Iversen, and so on in official documents: baptismal and census records. For the sake of both accuracy and clarity, let us refer to him for now by his birth name, Simen Bergersen, and just Simen while he is still a child; when he grows up and changes his

SIMON BENSON

name, we will call him by the name with which he became famous: Simon Benson.

Chapter 1: Early Years

Simen Bergersen was born 9 September 1851 in Gausdal, Oppland County, in south-central Norway, fifteen miles or so from Lillehammer. It was a small place with only a few hundred souls living there then, and it is not too much larger today. For a time in the late nineteenth and early twentieth centuries the community was divided into east and west, or Østre and Vestre Gausdal, but it was reunited in the early 1960s. Simen was baptized on 19 October of the same year. There is some confusion regarding the precise date of his birth: the date in September comes from local baptismal records, but Simen himself later claimed 7 October as his birthday, and this is the date that appears in the records of the cemetery where he is buried. It does seem rather odd to wait nearly six weeks between birth and baptism; one to two weeks seems to have been more typical in that time and place. For example, his brother Jon was born on 28 November 1843 and was baptized on 10 December of that year. Really, either date for Simen's birth seems potentially credible, though the written baptismal record carries more weight. His baptism presumably took place at the Østre Gausdal

Church, a Romanesque structure built of brick in the late thirteenth century and expanded in the eighteenth century. It would originally have been Roman Catholic but changed to Evangelical Lutheran at the time of the Reformation.

Simen's father Berger Iversen was thirty-four and his mother Karen Stenersdatter was thirty-one when she gave birth to Simen; he was the fourth of seven children. His oldest sibling was Jon, born in 1843; followed by Mathea, born in 1844; then another brother, Iver, born in 1848. His younger siblings were sister Stina, born in 1853; sister Gina, born in 1855; and finally, brother Kristian, born in 1859.

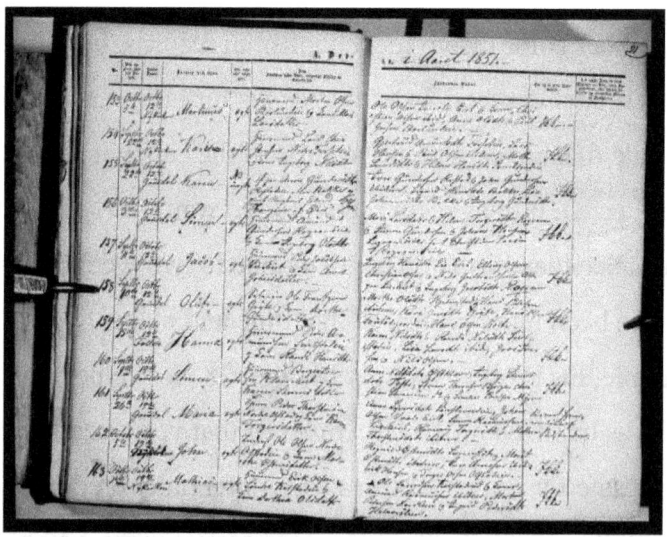

Simen Bergersen's baptismal record. His name appears fourth from the bottom. (National Archives of Norway)

SIMON BENSON

Gausdal is agricultural country, with farms from as small as a half-acre to as large as ten acres; most averaged one to three acres. Berger Iversen and his family lived on a typical farm of one and one-half acres. As an average farmhouse in that time and era, the family home would likely have been built of small six- or seven-inch logs placed vertically into the ground, supporting horizontal beam walls and a sod roof. The floor would have been dirt. The farm had a couple of cows as well as sheep, chickens, geese, and ducks. The family likely would have kept goats also. It appears mother Karen and the children took care of most of the farming while the father, Berger, earned extra money by doing general labor and carpentry work for neighbors. At that time land in the area was valued at sixty dollars per acre; thus, the Berger Iversen farm would have been worth about ninety dollars. A good farm hand, working twelve to fifteen hours a day, could expect to earn about six dollars a month. Simen and his family were poor, but not destitute; they appear to have been typical denizens of their rural community. However, one story told by a descendant of one of Simen's siblings illustrates how impoverished they were. At one point, the family was in dire straits and unable to pay rent. The landlord forced them to leave and locked them out – on Christmas Eve.

Fortunately, they were able to move in with one of Karen's siblings who lived on a neighboring farm. The sibling had the same landlord and allowing so many people into their house violated their lease, but fortunately the landlord never found out and Berger Iversen soon returned with enough money to cover the back rent. Interestingly, the land was owned by the local church and the landlord was Pastor Fleicher, the local Lutheran minister!

Simen later said of himself as a child, "I was always looked upon as a dreamer and a visionary. All of the rest of our family were intensely practical, but when my relatives and friends looked at me they shook their heads and said, 'Too bad, too bad; he looks at the stars in place of the ground.'" For example, "When I was a boy I decided that someday I would be a land owner myself and would own five acres." What an intriguing quote for a biographer of this man to consider! His family and friends were right to perceive he was a visionary, and in his life Simen would demonstrate that he had greater vision than they could have imagined: he had great, ambitious ideas that would take him far beyond that early desire for "five whole acres." Yet he does himself a disservice when he implies that he was not so practical himself. To achieve those dreams of his he always followed the most "intensely practical" methods.

SIMON BENSON

Simen would have received little formal schooling in Gausdal, perhaps a year or two of primary school at most. In the mid-nineteenth century, Norway was in the process of developing an excellent education system: after Norway gained independence from Denmark in 1814, its people recognized "that through the means of education, better than any other way, they could develop a people qualified to pursue the arts, to cultivate the science, to appreciate and enjoy the highest culture, and to maintain and develop their noblest ideals of citizenship and richest conceptions of statehood." Under the system that existed at the time, Simen would have begun his formal education at the age of seven. He would have attended a local schoolhouse or possibly he and other local children would have met with an itinerant schoolteacher who would move from place to place around the region. However, in his culture and era a child would have been considered old enough to support himself by the age of nine. He went to work full-time as a shepherd, then moved on to a job at a dairy where he milked cows in exchange for room and board. For a poor family like the Iversen/Bergersens, placing their children in other homes would have been a necessity.

SIMON BENSON

Nystuen: the Benson family home in Gausdal, Norway. (Photo courtesy of Ivar Lauritsen)

Whenever Simen and his siblings received any payment, they would give it to their mother to pay for basic living necessities. For many years, Berger Iversen and his family pursued the same dream as millions of other poor Europeans in the nineteenth and early-twentieth centuries: the dream of emigrating to America. To these people, America truly seemed the Promised Land. For many Europeans who felt oppression and bigotry, it offered religious and political freedom. For others, it promised new economic opportunity. For nineteenth-century Scandinavians, both social justice and potential to improve their economic situations provided considerable impetus. America was the land of their dreams.

A few Norwegians had come to North America during the eighteenth century, but the real "*Mayflower* moment" for Norway came in July 1825, when six families seeking to escape from the demands of the Norwegian state church boarded a small ship called the *Restauration* in Stavanger. Their voyage took fourteen long weeks, but eventually they arrived in New York City, where they were hailed by the press for their bravery. Local Quakers helped them establish a community in upstate New York, and soon word got back to the old country that the stories were true: they had found in America a literal land of freedom, plenty, and opportunity. In the early 1840s a man named Johan Reinert Reiersen became Norway's leading advocate for emigration to America. He founded a newspaper in Christiania (the earlier name for the capital city that eventually came to be called Oslo), and later a magazine called *Norge og Amerika* (*Norway and America*), which he managed to edit for some time even after his own emigration to yet another country, Texas, which would not become a state until 1845. Reiersen traveled widely throughout the United States and he especially loved Texas. In 1844 he also wrote a book called *Pathfinder for Norwegian Immigrants to the United North American States and Texas*. Letters "home" from happy Norwegian immigrants also began to appear in communities throughout Norway, and eventually some people returned to Norway to conduct speaking tours encouraging more emigration.

While for the most part life in Norway did not seem terribly bad for Norwegians in the nineteenth century, the country experienced the same political and social upheaval as the rest of Europe during the first half of the century, and other factors also contributed to the widespread urge to leave. People in Norway were living longer in the first half of the 1800s than they had been in previous centuries: the population's growth rate being greater than that of any other country in Europe meant land became harder to come by. In comparison, America was known to be vast and nearly empty; plenty of land was available for anyone who came to claim it. At this time Native Americans, like other non-white peoples, were not recognized as important or even as "Americans" in the sense of being citizens and members of society. The fact that they were in possession of all that available land would not have crossed the minds of the people being encouraged to immigrate. In general, sufficient quantities of food had been available in Norway because the Norwegians, like the Irish, had become great cultivators of potatoes. However, a severe famine in the late 1860s sparked a significant wave of emigration.

SIMON BENSON

Overall, these various factors led to some one million Norwegians emigrating to the United States between 1825 and 1920. Some sources say only Ireland sent a bigger proportion of its population to America.

Berger Iversen and his family focused their plans, their dreams, and their efforts to save money on their eldest son, Jon. This too was typical of families of the era who wished to emigrate. As the oldest (male) child approached adulthood, everyone in the family would work to scrape together enough money to buy steerage-class passage to take him to the New World, with the assumption that he would find work promptly and help the family save money to bring over the next child, and the next, and so eventually the entire family. Although it generally took a period of some years to bring the whole family back together in America, this process in fact proved an efficient model for letting whole families emigrate from Europe and begin new lives in America.

In 1861, the family had accumulated enough money – about fifty dollars – to pay for Jon's fare. Like many of his fellow Norwegians, he headed straight for the upper Midwest, specifically in his case Black River Falls, Wisconsin. Many Scandinavians began their new American lives in Wisconsin and Minnesota, and many chose to stay there; other immigrants, or their descendants, moved on to Iowa or the Dakotas, and some as we shall see made their way to the Pacific Northwest. Jon's decision to go straight to Black River Falls suggests he had some idea of what awaited him there: perhaps relatives or friends had moved there previously, or possibly he had heard of it through word of mouth. At any rate, his decision brought him into an entirely new line of work that would profoundly influence most of his family, including his brother Simen: logging.

*

The history of logging in the United States of America is the story of westward expansion writ small. It began in the forests of New England and the South and moved west as tree supplies dwindled and white settlers opened up more and more land to the west for development. In the East, early immigrants of course needed wood for housing, cooking, and heating. But even in colonial times New England developed a significant shipbuilding industry relying on terrific quantities of wood, and also started to export wood. By the 1790s New England exported some thirty-six million board feet of pine and more than three hundred ships' masts each year. In the 1830s, Bangor, Maine, was the world's major shipping port for lumber.

The call for wood became even greater in the mid-nineteenth century with the rise of the Industrial Revolution, which included the construction of railroads. Many steam trains used wood for fuel, though coal eventually overtook it, and also used millions of feet of lumber to make ties upon which railroad tracks could lie. Also, at this time, printers learned to make paper out of wood; previously it had been made from materials such as rags. Throughout the nineteenth century the demand for wood continued to grow steadily. The logging industry had to grow as well to keep up with the demand.

As forests in the East started to play out while demand continued to grow, the upper Midwest – Wisconsin, Minnesota, and Michigan – became the next hotbed of logging activity. Millions of acres of pine forests drew the loggers, including new immigrants like the Scandinavians, eager for jobs and ready to work hard for good pay. Logging ran close behind farming as the strongest contributor to Wisconsin's nineteenth-century economy. Interestingly, this Midwestern boom in logging came just as American popular culture started coming into its own. America was starting to develop a home-grown mythology celebrating its own legends, heroes, culture, and values, and someone found a way to include logging among the fields in which Americans should take pride. Tall tales of the gigantic, invincible logger Paul Bunyan and his massive blue ox Babe began circulating in the logging camps of the upper Midwest in the middle or late 1800s, though they did not appear in print until early in the following century. Unlike the folklore of earlier eras, the Paul Bunyan stories had so many humorous aspects they could never be taken too seriously, but in other ways they reflect the youthfulness and vigor many European-Americans felt as they claimed new territory in the New World as their own. The fact that it was not really theirs to claim rarely if ever crossed anyone's minds; instead, they just took what they wanted as their leaders egged them on with talk of "manifest destiny." The Paul Bunyan tales provide a good example to illustrate how the new arrivals in a region would create their own folklore and mythology to supplant that of the Native Americans who came before them.

Norwegians came in huge numbers to the United States; during the nineteenth century Norway lost more than ten percent of its population. Sometimes entire communities would shift from one country to the other over a period of years. While the largest numbers of Norwegian immigrants would not start arriving for a few more years, when Jon arrived in Wisconsin in 1861, Black River Falls was already a thriving community. Many of the new arrivals from Norway wanted to take up where they had left off, with farming. For others, however, especially single men looking to earn money to bring their families over, logging offered the lure of making good money quickly. A logger could easily earn three dollars or more a day in that time and place, and sometimes room and board were included as well. The logger would have had to do hard work for long hours, but it really must have seemed no worse than what he had done at home, and we must remember that in the land he came from, six dollars a month was the typical income. Even after paying for his own expenses, within four years Jon was able to send enough money for his oldest sibling, Mathea, to come to America too. She likely would have gone into domestic service. Two years after that, in early 1867, Jon and Mathea together were able to send enough money, some three hundred fifty dollars, for their parents and remaining five siblings to make the journey.

SIMON BENSON

It appears Jon Bergersen took no notice at all of the Civil War that was tearing apart his adoptive country at the time of his arrival. Wisconsin as a whole certainly did its part: more than ninety thousand young men went off to fight for the Union cause, and some twelve thousand did not come home. But for Jon and many of his fellow immigrants, the war must have seemed a distant battle, fought over matters about which he knew little; perhaps he even saw it as a boon: something that made more jobs available since so many men had left. Mathea also may well have not had much awareness of it. Like the Native Americans, the struggles of the African Americans, and controversies about their fate, would have had little place in Jon and Mathea's consciousness. And by the time the rest of the family arrived, the war had been over for more than two years.

*

Berger Iversen and his family set sail in the spring of 1867 and arrived in the United States after a voyage of five weeks. They did not pass through Ellis Island because it did not open as New York's great portal for immigration until 1892. Instead, their introduction to the United States apparently took place at the Port of Detroit, after sailing via

Quebec. Once the family arrived in America, they traveled directly to Black River Falls to join Jon. Berger Iversen promptly found work logging with his oldest son, but the newly arrived children did not. It appears the boys – Iver, Simen, and Kristian – took jobs as farm workers. This seems surprising: Kristian and Simen might have been considered too young to work as loggers, but at 19, Iver was the same age as Jon had been when he arrived in America by himself and quickly found a job.

The younger daughters, Stina and Gina, and their mother followed Mathea and found work as domestic servants. We tend not to realize nowadays how many American families in the nineteenth and early twentieth centuries had servants. Even a relatively modest middle-class home would have had a worker or two. They would usually be female, live-in domestic help as late as the 1920s and '30s: a cook and/or a maid, as well as a nurse or nanny for the children. Relatively few of these servants were American-born white women; those of them who worked were starting to find more and more jobs as teachers, office workers, and factory labor. In the South the vast majority of domestics were African American; even long after the end of the Civil War, few other opportunities would have been open to them. In the Northeast and Midwest, and elsewhere as other parts of the United States became more urbanized, one would commonly find immigrant Irish, Scandinavian, and German girls and women working as domestics.

Soon after their arrival in the United States, the male members of the Bergersen family made a significant change: they "Americanized" their names. Abandoning the patronymic system, they all took on the name "Benson." The boys also adopted standard English spellings of their first names: Iver apparently remained the same, but Jon became John, Kristian became Christian, and Simen became Simon. Thus, the subject of this book did not become the person we know today until sometime after his sixteenth birthday. Many years later, Simon Benson explained the family's decision:

> I believe that foreigners who come to this country should simplify their names for the sake of their children, and that they should become Americans, not in name only, but at heart also. They should learn to read and write in the tongue of their adopted country as soon as possible, and they should become citizens, for I believe that if this country isn't good enough to become a citizen of, it

is too good for a foreigner to stay here and make his living in.

To modern ears, in a country where many people celebrate their roots and previous cultures, such a call for immediate and complete assimilation might to some sound ridiculously old-fashioned and obsequiously trying to curry favor. Some today look down on efforts to assimilate. In Simon's era and after, immigrants from other ethnic groups – Irish, Chinese, Jews, Italians, Hispanics, and others – would have a much harder time gaining acceptance in America. They would face both official and unofficial discrimination that northern Europeans never had to experience. Some would take longer to assimilate; many, often because of societal

The newly renamed Simon Benson at age 18. (Benson family collection)

pressure and prejudice, would stay within their own ethnic communities, sometimes against their will, sometimes by choice. Some immigrants and their descendants continue to do so. Today they take pride in where they come from and continue to use the languages and customs of their former countries. But at the time and for people like the Bensons, happy to be in America and not facing much discrimination, the decision to assimilate was entirely rational and acceptable.

In 1918, Theodore Roosevelt said, "Every immigrant who comes here should be required within five years to learn English or leave the country." The immigrants of the era needed little encouragement: census takers in 1930 found the vast majority of foreign-born Americans – nearly ninety-four percent – had an adequate working knowledge of English. New arrivals in the preceding decades, like Simon Benson, loved their adopted country and felt eager and excited to become fully part of it.

The first farmer who hired the newly arrived Simon paid fifty cents a day, "which seemed like a fortune to me," he later recalled. However, the farmer also offered an extra incentive: he would give Simon an extra two dollars a month once he gained proficiency in English. Simon claimed that within three months he had learned enough English to speak it understandably and the farmer made good on his promise. This seems remarkably fast, although linguistic scholars have noted there are distinct similarities between Norwegian and English, beginning with their shared Germanic roots, which make English relatively easy for Norwegian speakers to master. Simon's employer also was likely sympathetic to this eager, hard-working young man; to add to his sympathy, it is also quite possible he was a fellow Scandinavian immigrant, or a descendant of one.

Simon worked up to fifteen hours a day on the farm and found time to study English on top of that. He recalled volunteering to take on extra duties consisting of morning and evening chores including milking the cows twice a day. By the end of his first summer in Wisconsin Simon had paid back the fifty-three dollars his brother John had advanced him for his fare and expenses in his new country. The following winter, Simon took a job at a different farm close to a school, with the understanding that he would work for room and board and be allowed to attend the school. This period appears to have been his final experience with formal education; however, his future writings and activities demonstrate he developed strong skills in English and mathematics, among other disciplines.

The following winter, 1869, Simon finally went to work with his older male family members in a logging camp. He took a job as a roustabout; the term denotes a worker with unspecified skills – that is, he was a general laborer. In the logging camp this would mean he would be expected to learn to handle any job in which he was needed, and indeed he came to master them all. For this he received eighteen dollars a month and board. He continued working in logging camps during the next several winters, and in the summers, he took jobs in sawmills.

And then things changed dramatically.

*

On 20 February 1876, at twenty-four years old, Simon married fifteen-year-old Esther Florence Searle, the beautiful daughter of Joseph Utter Searle and Jane Lucy Dalton Searle of Seneca, Wisconsin. Soon after, Simon opened a general store in Lynxville, a more substantial town not far from Seneca.

Esther Searle Benson. (Benson family collection)

Several questions arise here, and few answers offer themselves. Black River Falls is more than eighty miles from Seneca. How did Simon and Esther meet when they lived so far apart? One answer could be that Simon had taken a job logging or working in a sawmill near Seneca. At this time in his life, Simon would not have felt sentimental ties to a particular town or even family home. Sentiment was not something Simon appeared to feel strongly during much of his life. In fact, a single such home probably did not even exist. All the members of his family worked in camps or other people's homes, and his own life was somewhat itinerant, moving from job to job with the seasons. Perhaps a mill near Seneca offered better prospects, better wages, or better living conditions.

As an alternative explanation, he might have met her through his mother or one of his sisters. Perhaps Esther was visiting a friend in whose home mother Karen or one of the Bergersdatters worked as a domestic. There are other possibilities, of course; we simply have no way to know at this point, a century and a half later. Also, these explanations fail to answer the actual question: they explain how Simon and Esther could have come into proximity but not how they actually met. And further, how did Simon win Esther's heart? How did he persuade her parents to let him marry her?

Esther was a younger daughter, one of thirteen children, of a reasonably prosperous farmer of older Yankee stock. Simon at this time was a poor, working-class immigrant. What brought them together? What did they have in common beyond physical attraction? A photo of Simon at this time shows a handsome young man with luxuriant mutton-chop sideburns and mustache; in another photo, Esther is undeniably lovely. How did Simon woo her? How did he persuade her father to accept him as a prospective son-in-law? From Joseph Searle's perspective and the values of the era, Esther would certainly be marrying a man who, though certainly respectable, was distinctly beneath her. Social distinctions mattered a great deal in this era. The Searles would have seen themselves as occupying a position in what we now call the middle class. Simon would be well below that. Furthermore, while

SIMON BENSON

Simon at twenty-four was of average marrying age, Esther was considerably younger. Women in the 1870s generally married in their early twenties, but Esther was only fifteen, virtually a child still.

We have no answers, but somehow Simon and Esther won each other's hearts, and went on to have a successful if, sadly, a relatively short marriage.

*Simon Benson in 1876.
(Benson family collection)*

Immediately after the marriage, we suddenly find Simon the proprietor of a general store in Lynxville, Wisconsin, on the Upper Mississippi River just a few miles from Seneca. How this happened is another mystery. While it is not impossible he might have managed to start a business from his own savings, it is hard to think how he could have saved as much as he would have needed, probably some hundreds of dollars to occupy the store and stock it. As a likely alternative we may easily imagine the hand of

Esther's father Joseph Searle at work. It is not difficult to imagine him unhappy with the prospect of his young daughter married to a mere itinerant millworker and lumberjack. To make Simon respectable he could have set the young man up with a store of his own. Perhaps it was his wedding gift to the young couple. Here again, we cannot be certain this is what happened; Simon only said later that he "started a store." But why would a worker doing reasonably well in the lumber industry suddenly switch to running a store, an occupation about which he knew nothing? Where could he have come up with the money for such an enterprise and its inventory? Esther's father seems by far the most likely explanation here.

Joseph Searle died on 31 July 1876, leaving his widow and children a modest inheritance. According to Simon the store did well, and the prospering young family grew on 5 November 1877 with the birth of Simon and Esther's first child, a son, Amos Searle Benson. However, Simon had not insured his store, and in 1879 it burned to the ground. All of its inventory went up in flames, and the store's records too, so that Simon was not even able to collect any debts owed to him. He had little money. It became necessary to start over.

SIMON BENSON

Simon Benson was not a man who would give up anything easily. The setback of the fire left him feeling undaunted: "Losing your money doesn't amount to anything," he said, "as long as you don't lose your courage." Simon knew it was time to go back to the work he knew best, but he was also willing to gamble. The great pine woods of the upper Midwest were still strong, but he kept hearing that the real future of logging was in the vast, almost limitless forests of the Pacific Northwest. He decided to take his family to Oregon. By "raking and scraping" together every penny he could lay his hands on, he managed to buy tickets for himself and his family and set out for Portland.

… SIMON BENSON …

Chapter 2: Times of Trial and Tragedy

The United States in 1879 was growing rapidly, with a population of a bit more than fifty million people, but despite growth of some thirty percent between the 1870 and 1880 censuses, the nation contained vastly fewer people than are found there today; the nation's current population soars well beyond three hundred million. Along with such a considerably smaller populace, something we find difficult to comprehend nowadays is the sheer emptiness observers then saw in the North American continent. While we still have plenty of wide-open spaces in America, we do not have the vast, endless, unpopulated lands our forebears experienced. Even the more crowded East Coast would seem far quieter than today, and much of the West still had vast open lands. Native American settlements would have seemed tiny and localized, barely noticed or impinging on the awareness of people contemplating this vast continent-sized country. Moving west of the Mississippi one first finds hundreds of miles of fertile prairies of Nebraska, Iowa, and Kansas, then the mighty Rocky Mountain ranges, then hundreds more miles of rolling plains and high desert country. To the south lie the deserts of New Mexico, Arizona Nevada, and eastern California. Eventually, one reaches the temperate coastal regions of Washington, Oregon, and California.

The American states that border the Pacific Ocean are home to more great mountain ranges. A hundred miles or so inland from the sea stand the mighty peaks of the Sierra Nevada in California and further north the volcanic Cascade Mountains including Mt. Hood in Oregon and Mt. St. Helens and Mt. Rainier in Washington. Today these ranges draw millions of visitors annually with majestic beauty and year-round activities including climbing and skiing. They form part of the Ring of Fire, the huge area of tectonic plates and hundreds of volcanoes encircling the Pacific that make the region the most geologically active in the world.

However, other ranges of smaller mountains also rise along America's West Coast, known collectively as the Pacific Coast Ranges. These are not volcanoes but consist of sedimentary rock pushed up as a result of the convergence of tectonic plates that parallel the coastline. These mountain ranges run some one thousand miles from

SIMON BENSON

Southern California well into Washington. Similar ranges continue much farther north into Canada and southern Alaska for an overall length of approximately 2,500 miles. These mountains can rise to more than six thousand feet, but the average is closer to three thousand feet. In Oregon, the elevations run lower: a maximum of about four thousand feet and an average of fifteen hundred feet. From northern California to Alaska, their climate is generally mild and wet for much of the year. In fact, the regions can be so wet they are classified as "temperate rainforest," comparable in rainfall but not temperature to the lush jungles of places like South America's Amazon Basin. These temperate rainforests only appear in areas between forty and sixty degrees of latitude, and where mountains can catch precipitation while the ocean moderates the climate. "Less than one fifth of one percent" of the world's land can be classified as temperate rainforest. By definition, a temperate rainforest must receive at least thirty-three inches or rain per year, but many areas along the Pacific Coast Ranges receive far more: Astoria, Oregon, typically gets eighty-six inches of rain a year, and Forks, Washington, receives 110inches. Some more remote spots get still more: Laurel Mountain in northwestern Oregon averages 132 inches annually. Some locations in Alaska can receive more than two hundred inches per year.

*The northern Coast Range of Oregon.
(Wikipedia photo by brx0)*

The Coast Range mountains are not huge by the standards of the American West, but they are rugged and often difficult to cross. Today only a few passes cut through them, and in Simon Benson's day none did. Generally, riverboats plying the Columbia River provided what access there was to the sea and to coastal communities. In many places along the sea, a relatively narrow coastal plain only a few miles wide separates the mountains from the Pacific Ocean, but elsewhere they come right down to the sea and even into it. To the east of the Coast Range and west of the

Cascades lie the great fertile valleys of the West, including the Skagit Valley in Washington and the Willamette Valley in Oregon. Traveling eastward beyond the Cascades feels like entering a different world. Pine trees replace the firs of the western side, and the climate changes to high desert with low precipitation. In the east winters are colder and drier, and summers are hot; in the west the climate is milder and wetter all year round.

The Coast Ranges in northern California and southern Oregon are home to the famously enormous redwood trees; many stand more than two hundred feet tall, with a few reaching as high as 370 feet or more and standing more than twenty-four feet in diameter. They can live to up to two thousand years. The redwoods do impress, but they are relatively few in number and, in Simon Benson's day, they were not particularly accessible; even today, the areas where they grow are rather remote. Some logging took place there, but more operations grew up farther north. This is because there was better access along much of the Coast Range of Oregon and Washington, and because in these areas there stand millions upon millions of acres of "one of the best wood species in the world": Douglas fir.

While not quite as huge as its cousins the redwood and sequoia, Douglas fir (*Pseudotsuga meziesii*) can be quite impressive: one example in Coos County in southern Oregon stands at 329 feet tall and more than eleven feet thick. Even larger examples have been recorded. It may be the most common species of tree found in the Northwest, and certainly is the most common conifer: as many as eighty percent of conifers west of the Cascade Mountains are Douglas fir. The tree was first identified on Vancouver Island in 1793 by Archibald Menzies, a Scottish surgeon and naturalist who accompanied George Vancouver on his exploration of the Northwest coast; it is named for another Scotsman, David Douglas, a nineteenth-century botanist who visited Oregon and named many of its plant species. The trees can commonly live five hundred to one thousand years or more. They are, as one source says, "dinosaur trees": their genomes predate those of the great prehistoric reptiles.

Giant old-growth Douglas fir trees. (Photo courtesy of the Oregon Historical Society)

Native Americans used Douglas fir wood for small tools and its pitch for sealing; they also used the trees for medicinal purposes, believing they could alleviate headaches, stomach aches, and colds. When white settlers started to arrive, they quickly saw the tree's potential as a building material: the first sawmill appeared in the Oregon country at Fort Vancouver in 1827, and by 1833 Douglas fir was being shipped from Oregon to China. By 1849, records show some seventeen million board feet of lumber being harvested, and by the turn of the twentieth century the number would be in the billions. In 1947, nearly sixteen hundred mills would turn out seven billion board feet. After more than 150 years of continuous logging, Douglas fir is still the most commonly used wood everywhere: "No tree in the world produces more wood products for human use," says *The Oregon Encyclopedia*. In 1936, the state legislature recognized the tree's economic significance by naming it the state tree of Oregon. David Douglas brought samples home with him to Britain, and it is now "the second most common non-native tree species in Europe." It has become controversial in Europe as some conservationists see it as an invasive species, while the forestry industry considers it an outstanding product in its own right and a perfect replacement for Norway spruce, which has seen extensive damage from drought and insects.

Douglas fir's popularity comes from its strength: it is hard and does not wear easily, making it especially suitable for buildings and other projects, such as bridges and trestles, where wood that lasts well is essential. "It is one of the finest timbers for heavy structural purposes," says one expert. It also can be worked easily with machinery, and it dries quickly. Builders of houses and small commercial buildings love it. All wood needs to be allowed to adjust to changes in humidity before it can be used as lumber; this process is called "seasoning." Many types of wood twist or shrink or crack during while they are seasoning, but Douglas fir is an exception: it keeps its shape and size.

One of the great strengths of Douglas fir is its ability to grow quickly, but during the nineteenth century and much of the twentieth the endless forests of Oregon and Washington consisted almost entirely of "old-growth" timber – ancient, enormously thick, towering trees. These huge, old Douglas fir trees are largely gone now, replaced by second-growth and even later stands of trees. Early in the twentieth century, reforestation efforts were already underway in the Northwest. But before then, those original giants would make Simon Benson his fortune. When Benson arrived in Oregon in 1879, the logging and lumber industries were already well established in the Pacific Northwest, but the forests still seemed virtually infinite. The trees were there for the cutting, and America and the world clamored for wood for fuel and for building.

*

The state of Oregon has a distinctive character. Its people are proud of its natural beauty, its bountiful agriculture, its mild climate. People in the Pacific Northwest and especially in Oregon sometimes feel overshadowed by the sheer size, energy, and rowdiness of California and its population. There is an apocryphal, humorous story about pioneers heading west on the Oregon Trail. The story says that at some point on the route, the travelers would come to a signpost at a fork in the trail. The sign on the trail that went to the left showed a picture of a pile of gold, while the one on the right-hand trail had the word "Oregon" written on it. As a result, the foolish and illiterate travelers would head for the gold in California, searching for instant riches, usually in vain, while the sober, sturdy, literate pioneers would go on to start sensible new lives in Oregon. Oregonians are proud of their state's unique character and beauty and want to preserve it. In 1971, Oregon Governor Tom McCall told the rest of the country, "We want you to visit our State of Excitement often. Come again and again. But for heaven's sake, don't move here to live. Or if you do have to move in to live, don't tell any of your neighbors where you are going." While he did not refer directly to California, many people assumed that Californians were his real target audience. After all, he was just saying in a nicer way a phrase that was already popular in the state: "Don't Californicate Oregon." Beginning with the earliest era of mass migration of white people in the 1840s and continuing to the present day, Oregon has been proud of its singular character.

Which route from Wisconsin to Oregon the Bensons took is not known; Simon Benson only says he "bought a ticket." One possibility would have been for them to travel down the Mississippi River, then connect with the transcontinental railroad to San Francisco. From there they could take a steamship to Portland.

Another potential route would have been to take stagecoaches for some or all of their journey; stagecoach lines including Wells Fargo were still carrying passengers to and from areas not yet connected to the national railroad

The young Benson family might have taken the train from Wisconsin to San Francisco, and then a ship like this, the S.S. Great Republic, *to Portland. (Wikipedia image)*

routes and would continue to do so into the twentieth century. This would have meant a long and uncomfortable ride: one memoirist recalled, "Ruts, stones, holes, breaks, all combined to make this journey distinctly one to be

remembered. The alkali dust bit into the eyes, and one's lips cracked and irritated, hurt for weeks afterward." The train and steamboat combination seems to be the most likely method for them to travel if they could afford it. Train fares in third class, sometimes known as emigrant class, could have been as low as forty dollars per person; first class would have cost more than twice as much. The accommodations were spartan in emigrant class: wooden benches in cars that were sometimes pulled behind freight trains. Food, of course, cost extra. The steamship from San Francisco to Portland was surprisingly fast and efficient: an average journey took just a little more than twenty-four hours. *The Great Republic*, a typical steamship of the era, carried five hundred cabin-class passengers – what we would call first-class and second-class – and three hundred forty-six in steerage. Fares ranged from seven dollars for first-class passage to two dollars for those in steerage.

When Simon, Esther, and Amos Benson arrived in 1879, Portland had a population of nearly eighteen thousand people. This represented about ten percent of the total Oregon state population. Portland may have been a small city, but it was starting to take over and incorporate surrounding areas and communities: areas known today as neighborhoods or districts were once independent towns or unincorporated areas until Portland began to annex them. It had several churches, a growing professional police force, gas and water works, a new medical school; soon it would change from volunteer to paid firefighters. Journalists nationwide recognized Harvey Scott of *The Oregonian* as perhaps the most influential editor on the West Coast. Spring flooding on the Columbia and Willamette rivers would occasionally plague the city for decades to come; eventually dams were built along the Columbia, but the huge dams that tamed the river would not start to appear until the 1930s.

Portland was a "well-established and prosperous city." The California Gold Rush of 1849 opened a market for Oregon wheat and lumber products that would continue to grow, especially after Portland joined the transcontinental railroad network. It surpassed Oregon City, the previous largest city in the state, in the 1850s, and left another competitor, St. Helens on the Columbia River, behind with its superior access to the agricultural abundance of the Willamette Valley. The bridges crossing the Willamette and Columbia rivers, in which Portland now takes much pride, did not start to appear until later in the 1880s and early 1890s; instead, numerous ferries traversed the Willamette where it divides the city, while others connected Oregon to the Washington Territory across the Columbia. Wharves lined the banks of the Willamette through the downtown area and beyond, making Portland a hub of international commerce and ethnic diversity. Its "large Chinese community was second in numbers only to San Francisco's," and immigrants from all parts of Europe, like Simon Benson, would begin to arrive in significant numbers during the 1870s and 1880s, and its overall population would boom.

Of course, like every city Portland also had a darker side. The rapidly growing labor force created a market for unsavory amusements. Plenty of gambling haunts existed, and the Chinese quarter had opium dens. Business leaders happily reaped profits by providing space for such establishments. An unwary visitor who overindulged might even find himself waking up aboard a ship and forced to work; the secret tunnels through which men were "shanghaied" still exist today. Prostitution was also widespread. One madam, Nancy Boggs, even kept a floating bordello aboard a ship which could be moved to avoid raids by authorities. Rowboats took the patrons to and from the establishment.

After briefly getting to know Portland and checking into the job prospects, Simon left Esther and young Amos in town at the Overland Hotel and bought a ticket on a smaller local steamboat to the town of St. Helens, about twenty-five miles down the Columbia River. Near St. Helens the Coast Range mountains come down virtually to the banks of the river, and there the nearest logging operations could be found. Benson thought he might find work there, but he did not have to wait even the couple of hours it would take to reach St. Helens. During the journey, Benson fell into conversation with John Beavis, a lumberman who owned some timber land at Tide Creek close to Deer Island, a small community a few miles beyond St. Helens. By the end of the voyage, Beavis had offered Benson a job at forty dollars a month, not including meals. Even without board, he was already making approximately double what he had earned logging in Wisconsin; he must have impressed Beavis very favorably indeed. With his offering that amount, it seems probable that Beavis had hired Benson as a foreman or overseer for his Tide Creek logging operation.

Benson proved himself worthy of Beavis's investment. Within a couple of months, Beavis raised his salary to sixty dollars a month, and Benson could send for his wife and child to join him.

The Benson family's first cabin in Oregon, near Deer Island. (Benson family collection)

He had spent evenings after working for Beavis building a small cabin for Esther and Amos. He planted a large cabbage rose by the front door and a vegetable garden in the back. Some time later, in the spring of 1881, he was able to buy one hundred sixty acres of good timberland in the area for himself at five dollars per acre, making a small down payment and securing a line of credit for the rest. Large tracts of undeveloped land at that time were divided into sections of one square mile. One hundred sixty acres was a standard subdivision of land, known as a quarter section because it measured one-quarter mile on each side, and it was easy to break into even smaller units such as quarter-quarter units of forty acres each. The old promise of "forty acres and a mule" for freed African American slaves comes from the plans of William Tecumseh Sherman and Secretary of War Edwin Stanton late in the Civil War, and clearly refers to giving every former slave a quarter-quarter section of land; unfortunately, the Federal Government later reneged on the promise. Calling a distant corner of a farm the "back forty" also originates from this method of subdivision.

Benson's purchase contained six million board feet of timber. (A "board foot" represents a piece of wood one foot long, one foot wide, and one inch thick – altogether, one hundred forty-four square inches of timber.) A typical second-growth Douglas fir today can provide enough lumber to build up to ten houses; the old-growth trees of Benson's era stood notably taller and thicker. Back in Norway, this amount of acreage would have been twelve times as expensive.

Logging at this time was still entirely performed by intensive manual labor. In a typical logging operation, several dozen men would work, each performing specific, specialized tasks. "Fallers" or "choppers," working singly or in pairs, would cut down the tree with hand axes and crosscut handsaws which could reach sixteen feet long and were sometimes known as "misery whips" because they were heavy, difficult, and unpleasant to operate. The men would take great care to ensure the tree fell in the right direction to avoid injuring other workers, prevent the tree itself from breaking apart, and prepare it for removal from the area. Next, "buckers" would strip bark and branches from the tree and cut it into manageable lengths for hauling. Other workers would prepare the logs for hauling, attaching "dogs" to the ends of logs in order to attach them together to form a "turn" which could then be dragged through the woods.

Hauling logs over muddy ground and through dense undergrowth required use of powerful oxen; horses or mules might occasionally have been used, but oxen were preferred for their immense strength. (An ox is an adult bull that has been neutered for purposes of making it a docile draft animal. A steer is a young neutered bull. Loggers of the nineteenth century, including Benson, apparently used the words "ox," "steer," and "bull" more or less interchangeably to refer to oxen.) The chief driver of the oxen was known as the "bullwhacker" or "bull puncher"; he would use powerful shouts to guide the teams. In the eastern United States, loggers used giant wheels to haul their timber, but the soft, muddy ground and steep hills of the Coast Range rendered those useless in the Pacific Northwest.

Typically, five to seven pairs of oxen yoked together would pull a set, or "turn," of logs, though ten or more yokes were not unknown. A pole or tongue, as on a wagon, was attached from the forwardmost log to the rearmost yoke of oxen so the logs would not slide too fast when going down muddy hills. Pulling enormous loads through the thick Northwest mud proved virtually impossible; therefore, "skid roads" were created. Also known as corduroy roads, logging teams would create them by placing smaller logs, nine to twelve feet long and typically eighteen inches thick, perpendicular to the direction of the road. They lay several feet apart and were partially buried so that they looked rather like railroad ties. One worker, often the youngest, least experienced member of the crew and known as the "greaser boy," would liberally apply oil or lard to these skids; thus was the phrase "greasing the skids" invented to mean making one's path smoother and easier. The term skid road was later corrupted to "skid row" to refer to a bad part of a town.

The log turns were generally brought to the nearest deep river where "boom men" would sort the logs and form them into rafts for floating downriver to a mill. Sometimes the crew would put logs in shallow water and wait for the river to rise; sending large number of unconnected logs downstream was known as a "drive." Getting the logs into water as soon as possible saved much time and intense effort for the oxen.

All this describes a "typical" logging outfit of the time. Benson's outfit would have been much smaller, at least

Fellers taking a break from cutting down a tree. (Photo courtesy of the Oregon Historical

during the first year consisting of only himself and one other man whom he employed at thirty dollars per month. Benson's years of work in Wisconsin and his time with John Beavis showed him that he had mastered all the skills he needed to succeed in logging. A grocer in St. Helens extended him credit. With him and his assistant doing the logging and Esther doing the cooking, he started turning out product. He apparently had particular skill with the animals. Benson went to a man in St. Helens named Sam Miles and offered a deal: he would take six unbroken oxen from Miles and break them himself, training them to do hauling work. He would then either buy them himself or, if he were unable to do so, Miles "could get a better price for them as broken oxen than as wild steers." He managed to break the oxen within three weeks, and for the next few years he would drive them to the logging site before daylight in order to start work as soon as there was light enough to do so.

    Benson would stack the timber he had cut, then he would put the logs into the nearest river or large creek and bring them to the Northern Pacific Lumber Company. He was off to a successful start, and the success would continue for a time: "At the end of three years I had paid for my hundred and sixty acres of land, bought the three yoke of oxen, paid all outstanding bills, and had some money in the bank," he recalled. His family was doing well during this time also: 1881 had seen the birth of a daughter, Alice. The American Dream appeared to be coming true for the Benson family. They did not know that dark clouds were gathering on the horizon.

A felled tree after it has been bucked. (Photo courtesy of the Oregon Historical Society)

The most important tools of the early loggers' trade: axes, handsaws, and oxen. (Photo courtesy of the Oregon Historical Society)

*Oxen hauling a felled and bucked tree.
(Photo courtesy of the Oregon Historical Society)*

Loggers also had to be road builders: constructing a corduroy road. (Photo courtesy of the Oregon Historical Society)

*

Eighteen eighty-three started well for the Bensons. Simon was successfully finishing up his first major logging project. He had cleared his debts and made some money. His prospects for the future looked bright indeed. And then Esther was diagnosed with tuberculosis.

Tuberculosis is a bacterial infection caused by *Mycobacterium tuberculosis*. A man named Johann Schönlein gave it the name "tuberculosis" in 1834, from the Latin word "tubercle" meaning a small bump or swelling and the suffix "-osis" signifying a disease or abnormality. During the 1880s, Dr. Robert Koch identified the specific bacterium, for which he subsequently received a Nobel Prize. Throughout the nineteenth century and well into the twentieth, tuberculosis was commonly known as "consumption" – presumably because it caused its victims to waste away, "consuming" their bodies. Simon and Esther Benson would likely have known it by this name. Significant weight loss is one of the major symptoms of the disease; others include bad coughs producing blood and chest pains. It was once considered hereditary – there were even stories of people who died of tuberculosis then coming back as "vampires" to infect their family members – but scientists now understand it is transmitted through the air: one person coughs or sneezes and others inhale the bacterium. That bacterium lodges in the lungs. It may lie dormant for years, but then start to become active. Then it can spread via the blood or lymphatic system into the brain, spine, bones, lymph nodes, even the skin.

Tuberculosis is the deadliest disease of all time. The English writer John Bunyan called tuberculosis "The Captain of All These Men of Death." Medical historians have traced it back thousands of years to ancient India, China, and what is now Israel. The ancient Greeks called it "phthisis," and in Rome it was known as "tabes." The Greek medical pioneer Hippocrates considered phthisis to be the most widespread disease of his time. At its worst in Europe and the United States it killed as many as one in four people; even in the late nineteenth century, when it was identified as bacterial, it still killed one in seven people in the U.S. and Europe. It was the third most common cause of death in the United States, behind only cardiovascular diseases and influenza (which often led to pneumonia). Even today it kills about two million people worldwide each year. The bacterium infects between a quarter and a third of the world's population, perhaps two billion people; however, most have the disease in its latent or dormant form. Eight million are actively sick with it. A vaccine for tuberculosis has been available since 1921, but it is not always effective.

Notable victims of tuberculosis include former presidents Andrew Jackson and James Monroe; writers Jane Austen, Emily Bronte, Franz Kafka, George Orwell,

Henry David Thoreau, and Anton Chekhov; famous Native American Pocahontas; former first lady Eleanor Roosevelt; politician John C. Calhoun; actress Vivien Leigh; and composer Frederic Chopin. The heroines of the operas *La Traviata* by Verdi and *La Boheme* by Puccini both die of tuberculosis.

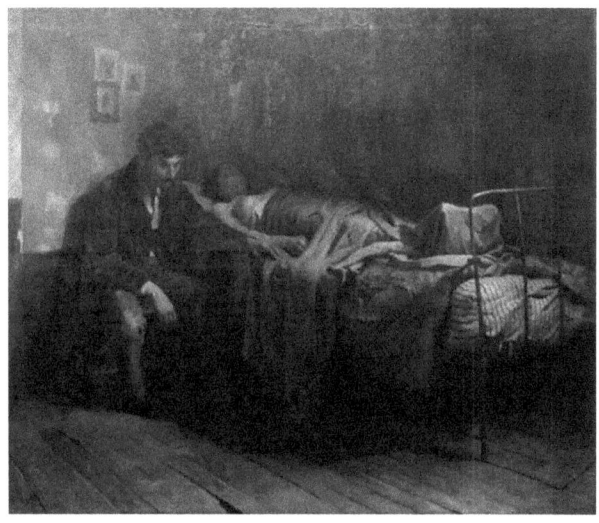

La Miseria, *1886 painting by Venezuelan artist Cristobal Rojas, who himself died of tuberculosis four years later. (Wikipedia image)*

Although the death rate from tuberculosis had started to decline by the late nineteenth century, so that it no longer necessarily seemed like an automatic death sentence, Esther Benson's diagnosis in 1883 was still profoundly grave news. It would change the family's life drastically. She had played a significant role in the family, cooking, doing chores, and taking care of the home for Simon and raising the children. She cooked for Simon's assistant as well. But everything would now have to change. The only way doctors knew to treat consumption was to relocate the patient to a dry climate. The Benson family would have to give up their logging business just as it was starting to take off. Simon Benson put his quarter section of timber, his logging equipment, and his oxen on the market; he received a total of six thousand dollars for the sale. With this he moved his family to Colfax, a farming community in the southeastern part of the Washington Territory (it would not gain statehood until 1889).

Colfax lies in the region of the Northwest known as the Palouse. This comprises much of eastern Washington plus parts of northeastern Oregon and western Idaho. Colfax was founded only a decade or so before the Bensons' arrival as a mill town, surrounded by good forests, but much of the Palouse consists of rolling semiarid prairie land which is now famous for growing wheat and legumes. Whitman County, of which Colfax is the county seat, leads Washington in wheat production and is the second most productive wheat-growing county in the nation. It is a national leader as well in harvests of barley and lentils. Colfax averages only nineteen inches of rain per year, exactly half the national average and considerably less than the more than fifty inches St. Helens, Oregon, receives. This was the dry climate Esther needed, something she would not have been able to find west of the Cascade Mountains.

The presence of a sawmill likely drew the Bensons to Colfax, and Simon took a job as a mill foreman earning seventy-five dollars a month. (Converting the value of money then to its value today is difficult and by necessity oversimplifies complexities of cost of living, but a safe rule of thumb would be that one dollar in the 1880s would have the buying power of about twenty-five dollars today. Thus, the job Benson took would pay less than two thousand dollars a month today.) This was not an enormous amount of money even then, although it was certainly enough to get by on; however, one must remember that much of the income was going to doctors' bills. Eventually, the Bensons decided Esther would have to go to work as well. She got hired in a millinery store – a store that sold women's hats. Life went on, and 1884 saw the birth of a second daughter, Caroline. This was still early in Esther's illness. However, her condition did not improve, and the medical bills continued to mount. She slowly started to waste away. By

SIMON BENSON

1888, Simon felt the only way to bring in more money would be to return to independent logging in Oregon, doing the work he knew best, and at which he had already proved successful. He began a difficult period of separation and several years of "commuting," living hundreds of miles apart from his wife and children, visiting them when he could, traveling a full day or more in each direction by train and steamboat, but spending most of his time in the Oregon Coast Range.

This time, Benson found opportunities to log along Beaver Creek, some twenty miles downriver from Deer Island and further up into the hills and inland from the Columbia River. He had enough savings to start an operation with equipment, oxen, and a crew of four men all sharing a small cabin. A 1916 article describes the one-room cabin as "rough and dingy"; another writer describes it as having walls "built of shaked, hewn sixteen- to 18-inch logs with split board roof." It was apparently still standing, little changed, nearly thirty years after Benson's time there. To help cut expenses, Benson himself did all the cooking for the crew on a stove he had carried in by hand because no roads then existed nearby. An elderly grindstone, which everyone used to sharpen their axes, stood outside the door; no one later remembered where it had come from, but it became something of a favorite fixture for the Benson crew. Another cabin, or shed, nearby served as a manger for the oxen. A nearby neighbor named R.S. Payne sometimes helped Benson with food and care for the cattle.

Benson's cabin near Beaver Creek. (Benson family collection)

In time, the timber was cut and ready to drive down the creek to the Columbia River. But then an unfortunate miscalculation led to a disaster that destroyed everything. The best place for Benson to put his logs into the water was upstream from a set of rapids known as Beaver Creek Falls. He planned to let the rising waters of spring carry them over the falls and downstream to the Columbia. In most years this should have worked, but this year proved an exception. Perhaps the winter had been unusually dry; perhaps there was less snowmelt than usual.

Log jam on a river. (Photo courtesy of the Oregon Historical Society)

For whatever reason, the spring freshet was unusually light, and it failed to bring the logs over the falls. Instead, it jammed them into the rocky ledges above the falls. The logs were stuck, immovable, with little likelihood that they would move before autumn at the earliest. Benson could not afford to wait around for several months, hoping his harvest could be saved. He had no alternative but to abandon the logs and move on with his life.

He made the long trip back to Colfax for a short visit, likely just a few weeks, then returned across the Cascades to Beaver Creek and found plenty more timber available for him to cut. Although the failure to capitalize on the timber harvest had left him virtually broke, he did not lose confidence. He knew he still had one thing to draw on to keep his hopes and dreams alive: he still had excellent credit with business owners who had faith in him. "If you're competent, your face can be worth a fortune," he once said. He had charisma and the ability to command trust in others.

Before he could start logging operations, Benson went to Portland in search of funding. There he persuaded a representative of the local office of the London and San Francisco Bank Limited to loan him enough money to meet immediate operating expenses. (The bank, while based in San Francisco, also had offices in Seattle and Tacoma; in 1905 it became part of the very large Bank of California.) It was located at 48 First Avenue in Portland and operated in the usual ways of the era, with enormous ledgers placed on tall desks; clerks seated on high stools would write everything down by hand in copperplate script. Customers' signature specimens "were kept in a big leather-backed book." Benson also received credit to buy supplies from Everding and Farrell. This company had started as a wholesale produce and commission organization, but later became noted for its connections to the timber and salmon-packing industries. Finally, he went to his old friend Sam

Miles in St. Helens, who allowed him to pay in installments for the use of four yoke of oxen.

Benson returned to Beaver Creek, where he had arranged to pay "fifty cents a thousand stumpage" for the logging rights to a particular area. While "stumpage" originally meant the price one paid per tree cut down, or stump left behind, by Benson's day and continuing to the present, it refers to the overall price of timber cut. Benson was paying fifty cents per thousand board feet. In return, he would receive several times as much upon delivery to the sawmill, although one must remember that Benson had to deduct a good deal to keep his business going: he had to pay for equipment, supplies for both animals and humans, and wages for his crew. As a general rule, Benson would have had to calculate using a complex formula: stumpage price plus cutting and skidding trees, plus hauling them into the river and transporting them to the mill, plus other fixed and variable costs. It was a tough business, but Benson had the backing he needed.

In fact, he would try his backers' patience. No matter how hard he worked and however long the hours he put in, when the loan came due, he was unable to pay it. According to his daughter Alice, on the due date he marched into the office of the London and San Francisco Bank, laid five dollars down on the counter, and announced that that was all he could pay. Somehow, he managed to talk the bankers into an extension and got enough time to pay off the loan. He always managed to come through in the end, and his creditors learned to give him the extra bit of trust he needed.

Benson had contracted to bring his logs to Ordway, Weidler, and Company, which had a mill near Cathlamet on the Washington side of the Columbia River. Ordway and Weidler must have offered him an especially good deal because there were certainly mills nearer and easier to reach from where he was launching them into the river. In fact, starting with this episode, Benson began a long and fruitful partnership with Ordway and Weidler; eventually, he would go into a business partnership with them.

This time Benson proved his competence as a logger and a businessman to everyone. By the end of 1889, his second season after returning from Colfax, he had got all his timber harvest safely to the mill and all his debts paid, including the bank loan. Furthermore, he had managed to put three thousand dollars for himself and his family in the bank.

SIMON BENSON

*

Esther Benson died of tuberculosis in Colfax on 28 September 1891. Benson was heartbroken. Noting that Esther's doctor's bills and funeral expenses had once again left him destitute, he said, "I was broke again. I was used to being broke so I didn't mind it, but losing my partner, that was a heavy blow, one that was very hard to recover from.... A wound in a pocketbook is much more easily healed than a wound to your spirit."

Twelve years after he arrived in Oregon, Benson was right back where he started, virtually penniless. He recruited his mother-in-law, Jane Searle, to care for Alice and Caroline. She had come to Colfax in 1881 when Esther became ill. After returning to Wisconsin for a time, she decided to relocate close to family or friends in Chehalis, Washington Territory, a small agricultural town west of the Cascades, almost exactly halfway between Portland and Seattle, directly on a train line linking the two cities. Today Interstate 5 passes through Chehalis on much the same route. The two daughters were sent to Chehalis, Caroline to live with their grandmother while Alice was enrolled in a nearby boarding school. At fourteen, Amos was old enough

SIMON BENSON

to accompany his father and learn the timber trade. He and Simon Benson returned to Oregon and work.

This time, Benson was determined to make a change.

Chapter 3: Innovation and Success

Esther Benson's death offered an opportunity for Simon Benson to do some soul-searching. At age thirty-nine, he felt he was no longer a young man. "His youth lay behind him," his daughter Alice says. "Sorrow helped mature him." A door had closed in his life, and he examined his career and prospects, looking for ways to open another. "I sat down at the kitchen table and with a pencil and paper I did some figuring," he says. "I decided to become one of the leading loggers and lumbermen of the West." This daring, ambitious decision may be seen as the real beginning of Benson's rise to wealth and fame; everything leading up to it was preparing him for this new start. His ideas included plans to go into a whole new industry and build his own "large and modern" sawmills: he disliked letting others make money from work he could do himself. He also knew he wanted to develop bigger and more productive logging operations. To become a leader in his industry, he would need to make substantial changes to his business practices, indeed, to make changes that would prove nothing less than revolutionary. He realized his plans would "require years of hard work, of courage and stick-to-it-iveness," and he had sufficient self-confidence to believe he could make it happen. This is the time in his life when we see Benson's deep belief in himself come to the fore. "I knew that if a man has a legitimate business, if he plans his work for the future, if he has faith in himself, if he will be square and work hard, he will succeed." Benson's belief in a strong work ethic, which he mentions repeatedly in his writing, helps to explain the success he would finally achieve.

Simon Benson in his forties. (Photo courtesy of the Oregon Historical Society)

Starting out again with virtually no money but with "assets of courage, intelligence, and energy," Benson returned to the same general area on the lower Columbia River. This time he found four thousand acres of prime timber near Cathlamet on the Washington side. It was owned by Julius Ordway and George W. Weidler, the partnership that ran the mill to which he had brought his timber for the last several years. Neither Ordway and Weidler nor Benson had the ready cash needed to exploit this property, but once again Benson had bankers and business owners ready to extend him plenty of credit, so he formed a partnership with the corporation's owners, each taking one-third interest. This operation grew quickly, expanding further into Wahkiakum County, where Cathlamet is located, and the partnership soon opened other camps, extending eventually to the densely wooded hills around Deep River, some thirty miles downriver.

Although most logging operations continued to be performed with manual and animal labor, Benson made his first major innovation at Cathlamet. He began to adopt the leading technology of his era: steam. While he did not pioneer the use of steam technology in logging, he used it in new and different ways, and adapted it to the special, difficult environmental conditions of the temperate rainforests of the Pacific Northwest Coast Range. He started his new era with trains.

Logging operators had understood the usefulness of railroads in their work for some time. Getting lumber from mills to cities and towns was an obvious first step: trains had started hauling milled lumber decades before. However, loggers had had to do their work reasonably close to rivers or lakes upon which they could float their logs to the sawmills. Oxen could haul felled trees out of the woods, but they could only bring so much timber so far; they could not haul large quantities of timber over long distances. Their slowness and limited hauling capacity, as well as the need to train, feed, and maintain them, made them fairly inefficient. Until recently there had simply been no alternative. Even several pairs, or "yokes," of oxen could only tug an enormous Douglas-fir log very slowly, no matter how well greased the skid road might have been. In contrast, a steam locomotive could haul dozens, even hundreds, of logs much faster. Eventually, cost-effective ways were found to bring railroad lines to the remote, rugged areas where trees grew in quantity, first in drier environments like eastern Oregon or flatter ones like the upper Midwest. Even in those places, however, trains were not universally popular among loggers. The steam locomotives of the era had enormous drive wheels that could be hard on the winding, twisting roadbeds in remote areas and mountainous forests, requiring frequent track replacement.

Benson bought a locomotive, likely at least second-hand, for six thousand dollars. He bought the engine "on time," agreeing to make payments until the debt was paid off, and he also found some old flatcars to carry the logs.

While in Portland he also bought second-hand steel rails – who knew one could buy used railroad track? – and built a mile-long line in the forest near Cathlamet. Benson said that single mile of railroad cost ten thousand dollars, which seems remarkable for its thrift and efficiency. The transcontinental railroad built thirty years earlier had cost sixteen thousand dollars per mile for the easy stretches and doubled or even tripled in mountainous regions. By 1890, the cost of laying track averaged fifty-six thousand dollars per mile. Of course, Benson had a workforce readily available, and all the wood he needed for railroad ties.

Benson's hard work, leadership, and bold investments proved remarkably successful. By the end of his first year logging in Cathlamet he had "paid up all obligations" and had managed to put twenty thousand dollars in the bank. The influx of resources that came from joining into a well-financed partnership with Ordway and Weidler helped him enter a new income bracket with great speed; however, alongside this we must also attribute his success largely to the excellent quality and easy accessibility of the timber at Cathlamet. He must have been able to oversee the cutting of a large proportion of that original four thousand acres in that first year, and he continued to log it in subsequent years. He did not just supervise, he remained always ready and willing to roll up his sleeves and work in any capacity in the logging operation, showing his crews that he knew every aspect of the job at least as well as they did.

The Cathlamet logging operation was good sized but not especially taxing for a railroad operation: the second-hand locomotive Benson had bought was a standard work engine that came to be known in the camp as "the Rattler," presumably for its noisiness and old condition rather than any dangerous snake-like qualities. A year later he extended the line and purchased another engine built by the Lancaster Locomotive Works in Pennsylvania. As he gained more experience with railroads, however, he decided to try something more ambitious, bringing a railroad line into the steep, rugged forest land near Deep River. The topography along the lower Columbia River can be extremely hilly and remote, making logging areas difficult to reach. For this harsh environment, he needed a special kind of engine: a Shay locomotive.

Ephraim Shay had been a physician, an engineer during the Civil War, and a store owner. In the 1870s, while running a sawmill and a small logging operation in northern Michigan, he determined that he needed a better way to get his timber from the logging site to the mill. In the upper Midwest, logging companies generally transported their logs in winter on large snow sleds, a choice that was not available for companies in the temperate Pacific Coast Range where snow rarely falls except on the highest peaks. Shay saw a need for a new kind of locomotive, one with gears that would allow it to climb steeper grades and that would make it possible to use smaller drive wheels that would cause less damage to the tracks. He began to experiment with designs, and in 1880, in partnership with the Lima Locomotive Works in Ohio, he built the first Shay steam locomotive. With various modifications, the Shay would sell in the thousands, especially to logging and mining operations which required the ability to climb steep grades and negotiate difficult curves. It would continue in use until the mid-twentieth century, an exceptionally long run. The last Shay was built in 1945, but many can still be seen on display or in use at tourist attractions.

The Shay is an ungainly looking machine, oddly different from the ordinary steam engines we see today in old photos and movies, or occasionally in parks. It

Advertisement for a Shay locomotive. (Photo courtesy of the Oregon Historical Society)

resembles a boiler sitting on top of a flat car, because all the wheels are the same size rather than having the usual locomotive configuration of smaller wheels in front ahead of two or three huge drive wheels on each side. Seen from the front, the engine appears lopsided, with the boiler set to the left rather than centered. This served to make room for a set of large pistons whose up-and-down motion sent power through bevel gears to all the wheels along the right side of the train, thus making all of the wheels drive wheels. This in turn caused considerably less wear and tear on the tracks, while the gearing gave the locomotive immense power. The Shay locomotive, and those built by other companies like Climax and Heisler, could haul immense loads around extremely tight curves and up incredible slopes. By 1892, Benson had bought a second geared locomotive, a Dunkirk-Gilbert built in Dunkirk, New York.

A geared locomotive like a Shay. (Photo courtesy of the Oregon Historical Society)

SIMON BENSON

Deep River provided outstanding timber for Benson and his fellow investors. As well as the supremely tall Douglas fir trees, the area also offered Western red cedar up to twenty feet in diameter, as well as hemlock and spruce. Photos from the era show trains hauling lines of flatcars each holding one single giant log. The old-growth timber is virtually gone from the Pacific Northwest now, and it is hard to fathom the enormous size of those original trees. The second- and third-growth is much smaller in comparison. Benson logged Deep River along with partners Adolph Olson and Richard Everding. However, he later sold his interest in Deep River when he decided to keep his operations closer together; Deep River was a wonderful site, but its location was too far away from his other camps in Washington and, later, in Oregon, and therefore not convenient for him. However, he kept an interest in the Deep River operation simply because it was proving so profitable.

SIMON BENSON

Train hauling extra-long logs. (Photo courtesy of the Oregon Historical Society)

Even as he enjoyed success at Cathlamet and Deep River, Benson kept looking for promising nearby areas of timber to harvest. His daughter says he was constantly "buying and selling both downriver and northward to Wahkiakum and Pacific counties; and upriver into Cowlitz County." On one of his frequent scouting expeditions, he discovered a "magnificent growth of timber" at a spot called Oak Point in Cowlitz County, just a few miles upstream from Cathlamet. Logging activity at Oak Point dated back to before 1850, when brothers George and Alexander S. Abernethy built a water-powered mill there. George had already become a significant early leader in the Oregon Country, serving as provisional governor of the region until it officially became a territory in 1848; co-owning the first newspaper west of the Rocky Mountains, the *Oregon Spectator*, using a press that had originally been brought to the Sandwich Islands by missionaries; calling for the founding of a militia, new roads into the Willamette Valley, and a pilot service for ships crossing the Columbia River bar; and donating to the foundation of the Clackamas County Female Seminary, Oregon's "first nondenominational school for women." Meanwhile, George Abernethy's brother Alexander stayed on at Oak Point, building a flour mill and a house and store along with the lumber mill. He lived there until his death in 1888. Today, Mill Creek and Abernethy Creek still recall this early development, as does a small cemetery where Alexander and members of his family are interred in a family plot. After Abernethy's death the timber property was available for purchase. Benson and his Cathlamet partners Ordway and Weidler quickly secured the stumpage at Oak Point for fifty cents a thousand and relocated their main operations there. Benson would see some of his greatest successes at his Oak Point operation.

However, before that operation could get well established, a terrible four-year Depression hit the United States in 1893. A variety of factors caused the depression, which also came to be called "the panic": dispute over the nation's currency and use of the gold standard, the weakening of the dollar abroad affecting balance of trade, farms producing more agriculture products than were needed. Massive unemployment and weak businesses resulted. With the price of logs falling, Julius Ordway developed a case of cold feet and decided the logging business was not for him; he did not believe the partnership could turn a profit. When the price hit a new low, dropping from six dollars a thousand to four with stumpage still at fifty cents a thousand, he sold his one-third interest in the partnership to Benson for ten thousand dollars. A year later, Benson also bought out George W. Weidler, who did not panic and held out for a much higher thirty-three thousand dollars. Benson remained optimistic and bought more locomotives and track; he opened a camp at Waterford, just a couple of miles from Oak Point. Unlike his partners, Benson was willing to gamble, and the risk paid off.

    Benson's operation at Oak Point quickly grew to employing some ninety men. The railroad made getting timber to the mill much easier, and he soon extended his lines. Trains were fine for pulling large loads of logs to the mill, or for hauling them to the river where they could be dumped in and formed into rafts. However, within the camps, oxen still did all the hauling work, bringing out the huge trees, often as much as ten feet in diameter or more, through dense underbrush from where they were felled, and towing them to collection points where they could be placed to await loading on trains. Loggers had to cut trees where they stood. Sometimes this would be on steep hillsides or in the midst of impenetrable blackberry thickets. Sometimes they would fall among debris from previously fallen trees or fires. Often the forest floor would be thick with mud. Benson saw a need for further change to get away from this difficult, slow, arduous process of bringing timber out and make his operation still more efficient. He decided to make another bold move into technology, one that had defeated other logging operators in the region.

    The donkey engine was one of those inventions that change the world that hardly anyone remembers today. It is basically a steam-powered winch: a cable that wound around a drum that used steam to pull far heavier loads than had ever been possible with the power of humans, horses, or oxen. John Dolbeer of the Dolbeer and Carson Lumber Company in Eureka, California, patented his donkey engine in 1882 and used it successfully in logging the gigantic redwood trees there. The machine consisted originally of a 150-foot manila rope more than four inches thick, attached to a drum; however, even stronger heavy wire cable soon replaced the rope. The donkey operated quite simply: basically, it would pull the log toward the engine with inexorable strength, dragging it through any intervening mud or brush. The temperate rainforest of the Coast Range has some of the most famously dense undergrowth in the world: thickets of blackberries and other bushes tangled among fallen trees. The engine itself could also be moved simply by attaching its cable to a strong tree and letting it drag itself through the forest on skids attached underneath. Soon more cylinders, multiple winding drums, and gears were also added to offer even greater pulling and lifting capacity. Donkeys could also be used to load the logs on trains quickly and easily. Soon the loggers gave names to different donkeys based on the role they played. The process of moving a log from where it was cut to the assembly point was known as "yarding," so the donkeys doing that job were called "yarders." Other donkeys pulled the logs down the skid road and were called "road donkeys." Crews would place donkeys at strategic points

Steam donkey engine. (Photo courtesy of the Oregon Historical Society)

along the road, then pass the logs from one to the next until they could be sent into the river.

The donkey engine found immediate success in various heavy industries that required pulling and lifting capabilities, such as construction, mining, shipping and longshore work, and especially logging in northern California. For some reason, however, the donkey had not caught on among loggers in the Pacific Northwest. Perhaps, as Alice Benson Allen suggests, they were just not willing to try new methods: "Old timers shook their heads and said, 'It is heresy to log with steam instead of men,'" she suggests. Perhaps those other logging operators tried to use donkeys but failed to use them correctly or efficiently in some way. Whatever the case, some of those other loggers had tried the donkey but turned away from it, while others had not been willing to try at all. Benson again had the know-how, patience, and self-confidence to stay with the engine and master its use, and in doing so he cut his operations' expenses dramatically. Suddenly there was no longer a need to build skid roads, thus saving on labor costs, and he no longer needed bullwhackers to drive the oxen and grease boys to oil the skids. The oxen themselves could be dispensed with, along with the costs of their training, feed, equipment, and maintenance.

Instead, after a tree was brought down by the fallers and then stripped by the buckers, a man would wrap a steel "choker" around the tree; he became known as the "choker setter." The choker "is a noose of strong cable (wire rope), which is secured around a log by wrapping one end of the cable noose to a bell [a type of hook] that slides and cinches around the log end." The choker was intentionally made smaller than the main winch line, so if anything became inextricably hung up, the choker would break rather than the more expensive main cable. Setting chokers was highly dangerous work and was often left to the most junior member of the logging crew. Logging in general could be extremely dangerous: in Washington at this time, the annual death rate in the industry averaged one death per 150 workers, and one injury for every five workers. In

*Logging crew with steam donkey.
(Photo courtesy of the Oregon Historical
Society)*

1920, the State of Washington would declare that logging was "more deadly than war." Even today, setting chokers remains potentially deadly thanks to the hazards of twisting, rolling, falling logs, or lengths of timber hanging up and breaking free.

After setting the choker and standing clear, the setter would wave to a flagman standing on a tall stump where he could see both the setter and the donkey. A wave of the flag would tell the donkey operator to open up the throttle and the engine would drag the log up to the assembly point. In time, the flagman was replaced by a "whistle punk" who would yank a cord to sound a steam whistle. The entire practice was known as "ground-lead" logging. Soon, however, Northwest loggers began developing further refinements. Demand for wood continued to grow along with the nation's population, and sawmills started to make improvements of their own, increasing their own efficiency. Even ground-lead logging was too slow to meet the increased demand. Early in the twentieth century, "high-lead" logging was invented and would become the norm. It is sometimes called "high-line" logging. This involved simply suspending the cables from tall spar trees. Doing this allowed the donkeys to lift the logs clear, high above the grasping undergrowth, and pull them to their assembly points. "[A]n industrial equivalent of a tenement clothesline," one writer has called high-lead logging. It is still used today, although the machinery now runs on diesel fuel, rather than steam.

SIMON BENSON

Spar tree for high-line logging, with steam donkey. (Photo courtesy of the Oregon Historical Society)

Benson soon began selling off all his oxen and replacing them with steam donkey engines, buying them cheaply second-hand from other loggers who had not found ways to use them successfully. He created what he called "the first all-steam logging show in the Pacific Northwest." Today it is difficult to say why Benson succeeded where others had failed, but he took excellent care of his equipment and learned to run the most cost-effective operation in the region as well as one of the biggest. He was getting six dollars for every thousand board feet of timber, and with the donkey engines he was able to lower his production costs from $4.50 to only $2.10. After the initial cost of buying the stands of timber, he was still making well over three dollars a thousand. In his first year he cleared seventy-five thousand dollars. He poured this back into his company, first adding more railroad lines and then starting to buy up as much adjacent land as he could get his hands on.

Steam donkeys could also be used to load logs onto trains. (Photo courtesy of the Oregon Historical Society)

Soon, the Oak Creek operation was broken into multiple camps with names like Bunker Hill, Waterford Camp, and Lower Camp. Each camp had a crew of thirty to sixty men logging, plus a small office staff, including clerks and a "bull-cook" in charge of keeping bunkhouses clean and, previously, feeding and caring for the oxen.

Some of the most important workers in the logging camps were the cooks, who could be either male or female. Loggers burned a lot of calories, and they ate huge amounts of food: sometimes as many as five large, calorie-heavy meals a day. In order to keep them happy, good owners of operations like Benson ensured they were some of the "best-fed workers in the country." According to an article on "the social history of food in logging camps,"

> A series of camps working about a thousand men around 1900 consumed half a ton of fresh meat daily, 200 pounds of smoked meat, a ton of fresh fruit and vegetables, 900 pounds of flour, 600 pounds of sugar, 190 pounds of butter, 2,880 eggs, plus unspecified gallons of coffee, tea, and milk.

Loggers working a ten-hour shift would typically consume up to eight thousand calories a day. Cooks would usually start their day by four a.m. One survey of a logging camp found an impressively varied menu: "corned beef, ham, bacon, pork, roast beef, chops, steaks, hamburger, chicken, oysters, cold cuts, potatoes, barley, macaroni, boiled oats, sauerkraut, fresh and canned fruits, berries, jellies and jams, pickles, carrots, turnips, biscuits, breads, pies, cakes, doughnuts, puddings, custards, condensed or fresh milk, coffee and tea." Clearly, good and plentiful food were high priorities for the logging crews, and cooks were beloved and respected members of the camp staff.

Camp crew of a logging operation. (Photo courtesy of the Oregon Historical Society)

During his time running and expanding the Oak Creek operations, Benson continued to work relentlessly to acquire more land. He recalled how closely he kept an eye on managing things:

> The other loggers said I was crazy and riding for a fall when I paid from fifteen to twenty-five hundred for a homestead, but whenever a homestead that

fitted into the district where I was working was offered me, I bought it. I was able to borrow all the money I needed, and I borrowed freely, to buy land and more logging equipment. One thing I insisted on: my bookkeepers must tell me at the close of each evening just how I stood, how much I owed, and how much money I had made that day.

Benson expanded his purchasing into neighboring Cowlitz County to the east. As his operations grew, he quickly came to understand the economy of scale: "I realized that the more cheaply I could produce [lumber], the more lumber would be used, and the more lumber used, the more money I would make." For him, growing his operations may have become an end in itself. Soon he found he was averaging twenty-eight hundred dollars a day net profit. When he started clearing three hundred thousand dollars a year, he felt he had achieved the complete success he had wanted: "I could make my dreams come true."

In 1895 Benson formed the Benson Logging and Lumber Company. The name of the business has interesting implications: he no longer wanted to run just a logging outfit; adding the word "lumber" suggests he was also ready to become a mill operator. For a man as ambitious as

SIMON BENSON

Benson, selling his timber to someone else who could earn more profit must have proved frustrating, even painful. He wanted to create his own corporation that would participate in and reap the benefits of all aspects of the forest-products industry. He took over the Abernethy Mill near Oak Point and tried to secure rights to build a railroad line from his operation to the mill, but he failed. This led to still another innovation: he built a long, steep chute, or flume, to send his logs down to the river where he could float them to the mill. Trains would drop logs from flatcars at the top of the chute. The logs then were sent down the chute at incredible speed: at times they made the thousand-foot drop in seven seconds, falling into the water with an enormous splash. In fact, they could go down too quickly. He once had to close the Oak Creek operation temporarily because recent rains sent the logs down so fast, they broke into pieces when they hit the river. He had to close the operation until the flume could dry. The logs would hit the water so hard, the sound could be heard across the Columbia River, easily a mile or more away.

    Not all camps sent their timber to the mill by this route. At the Bunker Hill camp, workers could roll logs directly from railroad cars into the Columbia. This might not have been as exciting to watch as the ones coming down the Oak Point chute, but it was certainly safer and easier, and Benson could appreciate both methods: "Mr. Benson could sit in his comfortable office at his residence, high on a bluff overlooking the Columbia River, in full view of both the Oak Point and Bunker Hill landings, and watch the giant logs splash into the Columbia." Benson also ordered an elaborate telephone system built that could keep him in direct contact from his office to every one of his camps.

Rolling logs from train to river. (Photo courtesy of the Oregon Historical Society)

*

Pamelia Loomis. (Benson family collection)

Benson would spend the next few years developing large and financially successful operations at Oak Point. He continued to run things from Cathlamet for a time, living in the former Abernethy house from 1895-1898. He also made new changes in his personal life: on Christmas Day of 1894 he married Pamelia Frances Loomis from Chehalis. She was a friend of his former mother-in-law, Jane Searle, and so already knew his children. Pamelia was born in 1865 in Beatrice, Nebraska, the daughter of Gilbert and Lydia Loomis, and came west with her family by wagon train in the 1870s. The transcontinental railroad had made cross-country travel significantly easier, but to move an entire family and its household goods, wagon trains were still the most practical and economical method.

Pamelia kept a diary of this journey, transcripts of which still exist in somewhat fragmented form. A typical entry reads: "We traveled 20 miles this forenoon. We took dinner 6 miles this side of Walkers ranch. We crossed the Platte where it only lacked 60 feet of being a mile. We camped at Kearney Junction." Another says, "We went across the Platte in a ferry boat that took one wagon at a time. Had to pay 3 dollars a team. We camped on Sage Creek. We traveled 10 miles today." Unlike the depictions we sometimes see in movies, the people in the wagon train almost exclusively walked the entire distance; it must have been a very long walk, especially for a child. All the space in the wagons was dedicated to cargo. After settling initially in eastern Washington Territory, the family was living in the Chehalis area by the 1880s. Pamelia graduated from the Olympia Collegiate Institute, a boarding school some twenty or thirty miles away, in 1889.

Benson's marriage to Pamelia was rather timely, as his former mother-in-law Jane Searle died on 1 October 1895 at the age of seventy-four. Thanks to Pamelia, Alice and Caroline still had someone to care for them. For the first several months of their marriage, Pamelia remained in

Chehalis, which had become something of a second home for Benson, but in 1895, perhaps because Jane Searle's death meant fewer visits to Chehalis, he moved himself, Pamelia, and his daughters into the Abernethy house at Oak Point and made that his new headquarters. Later, son Amos Benson would have a house of his own nearby on Abernethy Creek. His first wife, Georgia, died there in childbirth. With Pamelia, Benson would have two additional sons: Gilbert, born in that same year of 1895, and Chester, who arrived in 1902. Gilbert was named for Pamelia's father and shared his unusual middle name of Thereon.

Wedding portrait of Simon and Pamelia Benson. (Photo courtesy of the Oregon Historical Society)

Simon and Pamelia with their youngest son Chester, the author's grandfather. (Photo courtesy of the Benson Hotel)

Benson's daughters Alice and Caroline continued their schooling in Chehalis, Caroline now being old enough to join her sister at boarding school, and would join their father, stepmother, and brother at Oak Creek in the summer. Both girls would soon attend both Stanford University and the University of Oregon. A Chinese cook named Ming was also a member of the Oak Point household, although Benson insisted that the girls also help cook three meals a day when they were home, and he required them to can at least two hundred fifty quarts of fruits and vegetables every summer. Benson could be generous when he chose to be, but he well knew the value of a dollar and he approved of frugality and wanted to make sure members of his family could take care of things on their own. Thanks to his early days as a small logging operator, Benson himself was at least a competent cook as well. Alice recalls going on trips with him to "cruise timber" – that is, inspect his holdings or look for potential new stands to buy – during which Benson would use a special portable stove to make "hot cakes and bacon and eggs for breakfast, and fresh fish for dinner."

While most of her memories seem idyllic, Alice also shares a more exciting and dangerous memory. In the summer of 1896 while she was home for vacation, a great forest fire swept toward Oak Point. At first Benson hoped his camp would be spared, but a shift in the wind brought it straight in. Benson managed to lead about one hundred fifty men, women, and children, including his own family, to safety, first walking them up the railroad tracks and over trestles, then climbing a rope ladder down a cliff to the safety of the river. Alice recalls her own terror but says her father remained calm and kept everyone from panicking. The only ones who did not survive were a pair of saddle ponies belonging to Alice and Caroline: they started to follow but refused to walk onto the first trestle. The fire forced the closure of the Oak Point camp for the rest of the summer as it destroyed the chute and roadway, and even sent some railroad track into the river. Everything had to be rebuilt.

By now, Benson was developing a reputation across the country and even internationally as the rest of the world started to discover the outstanding quality of the Douglas fir as a building material. Benson could demand top dollar for his lumber, as much as twelve dollars per thousand for the best parts when the typical rate was only a fraction of that. He developed a specialty in selling custom logs for specific purposes; for example, in 1899 he fulfilled an order to send a 150-foot flagpole to Yokohama, Japan. A local newspaper said of it, "The stick measures 150 feet in length, 28 inches at the butt, and 15 inches at the top." Special means were needed to transport such extra-long logs: they could not fit on ordinary railcars or be hauled around ordinary curves in the track. Pictures show immense "Benson long logs" of more than one hundred feet with each end on a small flatcar and free in the middle. The middle portion would actually sag under the logs' tremendous weight. Instead of dealing with curves, "switchbacks" sent these "sticks" on unconnected cars back and forth rather than trying to turn them. At each switchback, the geared engine would simply change direction and move on up to the next level.

"No success comes by chance," Benson is quoted as saying. By 1899, his operation had twelve miles of railroad track, several locomotives, hundreds of loggers, office staff, cooks, and other camp workers. That year his company cut some forty million board feet of timber. In 1901, the company bought three more Shay locomotives, bringing its total number of locomotives to eight, of which six were Shays. Yet Benson himself had taken a step back and was no longer directly overseeing the operation. In 1898, he decided to move his family to Portland, leaving Amos, now in his twenties, as the manager on the spot. With so many successes, so much money coming in, so many dreams fulfilled, Benson may have had some thoughts about retirement, though for a man with his energy and not yet fifty years old, this seems unlikely. He continued to visit Oak Point frequently, and as we will see, he would soon find plenty of other activities to occupy himself.

*

Portland at the turn of the twentieth century was a bustling place. It had changed immensely from the town Benson had first seen only twenty or so years before.

SIMON BENSON

Portland's population had virtually doubled in the last decade of the nineteenth century, climbing from forty-six thousand to ninety thousand in 1900; in the first ten years of the twentieth century it would more than double again to over two hundred thousand. It had the busiest port on the West Coast north of San Francisco, although Seattle would soon surpass it when the Alaska Gold Rush, a deep-water port, and better rail access spurred greater increases in business. Seattle's surge in growth from 1900-1910 was even greater than Portland's: it went from about eighty thousand to nearly two hundred forty thousand. Portland grew largely thanks to the great waves of immigrants who came to the United States during this period. The city saw influxes of people from Japan, China, the Scandinavian countries, Britain and Ireland, Canada, and Germany. Smaller groups arriving in Portland included Italians, Jews from eastern Europe, Croatians, and African Americans from the Southern states. We must attribute much of this growth to the general rise of immigration to the United States in the late nineteenth century, and some also to Portland's joining the national railroad network in 1883.

SIMON BENSON

Scenic views of Portland, 1890. (Photo courtesy of the Oregon Historical Society)

Immigration from foreign countries and other parts of the United States explains much of Portland's population boom around the beginning of the new century, but annexation also played a significant role. When Benson first arrived, numerous small villages surrounded Portland, which people had only recently stopped referring to as "Stumptown" because the original town, what is now the downtown area, grew so quickly, no one could be bothered to remove the stumps. Now, many of those surrounding villages had been swallowed up and brought into the city. Much of what is now in the quadrants of Southwest,

Northwest, Southeast, Northeast, and North Portland originally consisted of separate towns like Sellwood, Albina, and East Portland.

After the depression of the 1890s, business began to boom again in Portland and throughout the nation. Portland in particular benefitted from increased trade with Pacific and Asian lands: Hawaii, which had been annexed as a U.S. territory in 1898, as well as China, Japan, and the Philippines. Benson's daughter Alice especially remembers the amazing selection of teas available in Portland, and that coffee and spice businesses also did very well. Even earlier, by the 1880s, mills in Portland were sending wood products as far afield as Central America, Peru, Chile, and Australia. Portland's shipyards throve too, especially in the construction of steamboats, steam-powered tugboats, and smaller craft for use on the Columbia and Willamette rivers. Farther down the Columbia, fish canneries continued a boom that had started decades earlier. Rudyard Kipling wrote an essay on canning on the Columbia in 1889 during an American tour. Kipling, not known for his enlightened views on race, noted that the canneries only employed "Chinamen" who "looked like "blood-besmeared yellow devils." In 1903, however, the majority of these workers would lose their jobs when a new piece of technology, unfortunately named the "Iron Chink," was developed to decapitate and clean fish; its rotating brushes and blades could replace fifty workers. Salmon at this time did not have the exalted place it enjoys now in the world of seafood lovers. Consumers then saw it as junk fish, much as people today view canned tuna. The number of salmon, rather like the vast forests of Douglas fir, seemed endless, their supply unending, and therefore the fish were considered nothing special. One modern Oregonian recalls her grandfather relating stories from his youth of taking a horse-drawn wagon to the Sandy River – a tributary of the Columbia – and using a pitchfork to fill the wagon with migrating salmon, then taking it back to his family's farm and sowing the fields with fish as fertilizer.

Along with lumber and canned fish, wheat became another major export from Portland to the rest of the world. The expansion of the railroad networks throughout the Northwest made bringing wheat to Portland easier. One Portland mill recorded an average daily output of eight thousand barrels, or nearly eight hundred tons; the Portland Grain Company was "exporting forty to fifty thousand tons a year" early in the twentieth century. Today, Portland remains the Unted States' leading exporter of wheat and stands among the top ports for exporting other agricultural products, including grains, soybeans, vegetables, and berries. Thirty-five percent of the country's wine exports also pass through the Port of Portland.

Portland in the 1890s. (Photo courtesy of the Oregon Historical Society)

Labor unions had been gaining strength for some time in Portland, and in 1890 some locals, led by the carpenters' unions, joined a national strike demanding an eight-hour workday and closed shops. An enormous rally on May Day forced the Portland Builders Exchange to settle. Ten years later, unions remained strong in Portland. This likely had a profound influence on Benson, who was deeply conservative and though he recognized the power, possibly the necessity, of unions – he once predicted that someday there would likely be a "labor president" – he was not really friendly to the union movement. He believed in treating his workers well, but he also believed he should be in charge and wanted no part of what he perceived as being told what to do by his employees.

With all the shipping going in and out of Portland, the dark side of the city continued to prosper. Sailors and others looking for fun in the area along the waterfront could easily find liquor and carnal entertainment, but as we saw previously, they also risked being shanghaied: drugged or knocked unconscious and dragged aboard a ship that needed hands, to wake up hours later and far out to sea, forced to work and go wherever the ship took them. Shanghaiing was such a major enterprise that a network of tunnels developed under the streets and buildings in the Old Town and adjacent Chinatown areas of Portland, close to the waterfront. For this reason, some visitors referred to Portland as the "Unheavenly City."

Like every nineteenth-century city that had pretensions of glory, Portland had a thriving cultural scene. Philip Marquam's Grand Opera House had opened in 1890. It boasted more than fourteen hundred seats and some eight hundred electric lights. The first performance there was of Gounod's *Faust*. Other theaters in Portland also offered opera as well as concerts, vaudeville, and even boxing exhibitions. The Portland Art Museum was founded in 1892 and originally located in the public library. The Oregon Symphony formed in Portland in 1896; today it claims to be the oldest such institution west of the Mississippi River. And even in this relatively early period in the city's history, people had already started to appreciate the region's interesting past: the Oregon Historical Society was founded in 1898. When Benson relocated to Portland with his family in 1898, it had all the facilities and trappings of any significant American city. A large network of interurban trains, steam and electric trolleys, and even San Francisco-style cable cars spread across the city and into the suburbs. People could commute miles from home to work, rather than walk as they had in the past.

Benson continued to visit Oak Point often, but it seems clear he quickly fell in love with Portland and wanted to make it his permanent home. After renting a house on Southeast Belmont Street for a couple of years, in 1900 he oversaw construction of the house that still bears his name to this day. It was located on an extra-large corner lot at Southwest Eleventh Avenue and Clay Street. It is a beautiful Queen-Anne style building, richly decorated, with interesting curved front windows and different kinds of wood paneling in every room. Benson's youngest son,

Chester, was born in the house, and Simon Benson would continue to live there until 1913, after his marriage to Pamelia had ended in divorce. No records or reminiscences of their marriage survive, but perhaps she did not love the relatively big-city life of Portland, as he did. Perhaps he did not find her supportive or lively enough to suit his developing celebrity. Or perhaps she resented the considerable amount of time he was spending away from home.

Benson was spending a good deal of time traveling, not only visiting Oak Point but also exploring new possibilities for expanding his business. In 1900, he returned to Black River Falls, Wisconsin, for a visit. He also traveled frequently to California and other destinations, likely including Chicago and possibly New York. Also, for some time he had been buying large tracts of land around Clatskanie, Oregon, a small town on the Columbia River across from Oak Point and Cathlamet. The railroad connecting Portland to Astoria on the coast had been completed in 1898 and stopped at Clatskanie, making it convenient as well as a promising site to cut timber. A local newspaper reported on 29 May 1902,

SIMON BENSON

Simon Benson, the Oak Point logger, has lately purchased some 5,000 acres of timber land back of Clatskanie. When he has exhausted the timber in which his logging camps are now situated, near Oak Point, he will build eight miles of railroad from Clatskanie to his new purchase and commence logging the timber off.

Benson would move his operation to Clatskanie using his own work boats to ferry workers and equipment. He had a "fleet" of three boats: the *Mountain Maid*, the *Mountain Rose*, and the *Mountain Belle*. He started the camp with two locomotives and two donkey engines, but as he had done at Oak Point, he quickly expanded his operations far beyond those eight miles of railroad as he purchased more land from homesteaders who were happy to sell their holdings because Benson was willing to pay well for them. As he had at Oak Point, Benson looked for landowners with four to seven million board feet of timber on their land. An associate named Billie Congers helped him with property purchases: he became friendly with homesteaders, hunting and fishing with them, and steering them to Benson when they were ready to sell. Benson eventually owned several times that original five thousand

The Simon Benson House, still standing today on the campus of Portland State University. (Photo by author)

acres and built a huge operation around Clatskanie very quickly; he said later that he would make "most of his money" there.

The operations at Clatskanie – the town's name derives from the Tlatskanai Native American tribe and is pronounced "CLATS-kuh-nigh" – soon consisted of five locomotives on a rail network that, including branches and switchbacks, covered nearly eighty miles; twenty donkey engines; and some two hundred fifty workers in nine separate camps with names like Erickson and Keystone. Many of the former railroad grades, long since shorn of their rails and ties, now serve as trails for hiking, hunting, and fishing. Meanwhile, his former holdings around Clatskanie still continue to produce timber, although the old camp facilities are long gone. A single wigwam burner, a large structure used to burn off waste materials from mill operations, still stands, long disused and quite overgrown, on the bank of Beaver Slough. The main camp was located at Swedetown, on the edge of the Clatskanie town center. Benson also built what may have been his first truly "large and modern" mill at Clatskanie, bigger and better than the Oak Point facilities, again finding it preferable to make money from all aspects of the logging and lumber business from beginning to end, felling the tress to turning out high-quality milled lumber products. Although Amos was in charge of the Clatskanie front-office operations in place of the nominally retired Simon, a man named William Kidney served as general superintendent and did much of the actual managing.

SIMON BENSON

Log flume at Clatskanie. (Photo courtesy of the Oregon Historical Society)

Benson cultivated a reputation as a good employer and especially liked to hire Scandinavian immigrants like himself. Many spoke little or no English and did not share his remarkable skill at adapting to a new language, so they wore badges saying "Simon Benson Camp" so townspeople would recognize their limitations and know if they needed to be guided through shopping or getting back to their quarters. He fed his workers well and paid them regularly when smaller operators often had to make their men wait until their logs had sold. He paid slightly higher wages than most operators, to keep his workers happy, and he made sure always to have the newest and best equipment in his camps. He even offered an early, primitive form of health insurance coverage, charging employees seventy-five cents a month for doctor and hospital costs. In a high-risk field like logging, this was a rare perquisite and much appreciated.

Life in a logging-camp bunkhouse. (Photo courtesy of the Oregon Historical Society)

Benson continued to live in Portland and officially Amos was the operations manager; he had a house built for Amos in Clatskanie near the company's headquarters. It still stands today. However, it seems clear Simon Benson continued to spend a good deal of time on the scene. He considered Clatskanie his best, most successful, and most lucrative operation, the one in which he took the most pride. And he was beginning to plan a new innovation that would stand as his greatest triumph of all.

Amos Benson on a company train in front of his house in Clatskanie. (Photo courtesy of James Aalberg)

SIMON BENSON

Chapter 4: Crowning Enterprise: The Rafts

The great building boom that started Los Angeles on the path to the vast urban conglomeration we know today began in 1885. In that year, the Atchison, Topeka, and Santa Fe Railway Company completed its transcontinental line to San Diego; two years later it arrived in Los Angeles. This broke a monopoly on rail travel in and out of the region previously held by the Southern Pacific and started a fare war. Passenger rates actually dropped from more than $100 to as low as $1 for the trip from St. Louis or Kansas City to Los Angeles or San Diego, and people came in droves to the supposed new "promised land" of sunshine and fresh fruit year-round. Promoters publishing books and articles about the "Mediterranean climate" and bounteous farmland helped encourage the immigrants. In 1887 alone, as many as 120,000 people came to Southern California, some just to visit and some to stay, and that was only on the Southern Pacific line.

SIMON BENSON

In 1880, Los Angeles had a population of eleven thousand; in 1890 it had more than quadrupled to fifty thousand; by 1900 it had doubled again to 102,000; within another five years it had surpassed two hundred thousand. And by 1910, Los Angeles had grown to a staggering nearly 320,000. San Diego showed at least as remarkable growth: in a single eighteen-month period from 1885-87, its population grew from approximately five thousand to some forty thousand. Growth in the many towns and cities in the areas surrounding Los Angeles and San Diego was comparable. For example, Riverside County, which is listed as having virtually no population at all in 1890, by 1910 contained almost thirty-five thousand souls. (An enormous frenzy like this could not last, and perhaps ten thousand of those new arrivals to San Diego soon left disappointed, often after losing their money to overzealous real-estate speculation, but both Los Angeles and San Diego, as well as their surrounding areas, were by then well established and bound to continue growing.)

Such uncontrolled growth of course caused overwhelming pressure to provide resources: roads, rail transportation, electricity, and most of all, water. The insatiable need for water at this time caused Southern Californians to begin building an enormous aqueduct, thus beginning the area's long tradition of taking – or stealing – water from the rest of the Southwest. Even today, some in the region still cast a covetous eye on the Columbia River and there have been serious proposals to build a pipeline one thousand miles long or more to bring water to Southern California from Oregon, Washington, British Columbia, and even Alaska.

Simon Benson at the turn of the twentieth century. (Benson family collection)

Farther north, as we have already seen, Portland was also continuing to grow steadily. Its size would double from 1890 to 1900, and more than double again to two hundred thousand by 1910. Also, by 1910, Seattle would surpass Portland in population and never look back. The entire West Coast of the United States was growing at a ferocious pace, in spite of the terrible economic depression that hit the nation in the mid-1890s.

SIMON BENSON

Along with the rest of the country, Simon Benson watched what was going on. He must have been as amazed as everyone else by the sheer enormity of the terrific growth that was going on, especially in California, though perhaps he was not completely surprised. He frequently visited San Francisco on business. His daughter says he had "always been fond of sunny California," and she remembers many visits farther south to places like Palm Springs and Long Beach where he would have seen for himself the pleasant Mediterranean climate of the Southland. And Benson would have watched all that growth with an eye focused especially on the need for one resource in particular: building materials for houses, the wood he had for sale. He became obsessed with finding a practical, affordable way to get his logs to Southern California.

Portland would continue to be a fine market for Benson lumber products. Benson's adoption of modern technology allowed him to compete effectively with other logging outfits in the region. In Washington, Weyerhaeuser only began to build his huge operations in 1900; it would take some years for it to grow into a threat – and besides, it was well to the north in Tacoma. Only in 1905 would Washington surpass Oregon in timber production; Oregon would later take the lead back. Benson could concentrate on the Portland market as well as national and international trade. But just as he had looked to the future in 1879 when he chose to leave Wisconsin and found it in the vast timberlands of the Northwest, now he looked again and this time his gaze was drawn to the south. All those people coming to California needed places to live, but who would build them, and with what? Southern California was not known for its lush forests; the wood for all those houses, stores, churches, and schools would have to come from somewhere else. But where? Why not Oregon?

Benson knew there was a huge and rich market waiting there in the arid, semi-desert Southland and he wanted to get into it. But this raised another, much larger question: How? How could he get enough lumber to Los Angeles and San Diego to make a worthwhile profit in that burgeoning market?

The problem was shipping: carrying the lumber to a market some one thousand miles away. Benson had two options. He could load it all onto flatbed rail cars and pay for the railroad company to carry it, or he could put it on ships and send them down the coast, paying the shippers. Both choices were forbiddingly expensive and labor intensive. He would have to see every log loaded individually by crane and then pay for each heavy log to be carried by some railroad or shipping company. The companies charged using a formula based on the cost of carrying a ton of freight for one mile, and a typical log might weigh several thousand pounds. Shipping large quantities of lumber over such a long distance was an extremely cost-prohibitive proposition. Also, ships at the time could only carry relatively small loads of timber, compared to the amount needed in Southern California, and ship owners charged more because such loads were dangerous: they could shift easily, endangering the entire vessel. Many of the logs coming out of Benson's logging camps were too large for ships of the time as well.

"One thing I could not seem to solve and that was how to get my lumber to California more cheaply," Benson said. "I could not control the freight rate." This quote illustrates Benson's desire to minimize costs and maximize profits, but it also offers another factor to consider. Benson liked to keep as much control of his operations as possible. He was confident in his abilities and competence; he believed in himself. He would always prefer to keep his products in his own hands as much as he could, and he did not like letting anyone else have control over any aspect of his operation.

But how could he do that in this case?

Benson, after "long and deep study," realized the obvious answer was to raft the lumber, but that was not a simple solution. Logging outfits had rafted their harvests on rivers for centuries, even millennia. It was simply a matter of floating the logs and tying them together or, later, surrounding them with a log boom linked together with chains. Before technology allowed lumbermen to use railroads in their hard-to-reach locations far from civilization, floating logs on rivers was the only realistic way to get cut logs to mills. Even after trains came into use, loggers still often used them to take their timber only as far as the nearest suitable waterway. Log rafts were still the most efficient and cheapest way to bring out logs, and they were also used to transport many other types of goods.

SIMON BENSON

A typical log raft on a river. (Photo courtesy of the Oregon Historical Society)

Rafting logs on rivers has a long and storied history which continued well into modern times. The author can remember seeing tugboats towing log rafts regularly plying the Willamette River through Portland at least into the 1970s; the mills at Oregon City started shutting down in the 1980s, thus ending the log rafting on the lower Willamette. However, Benson faced an entirely different proposition when it came to rafting timber on the sea. The ocean is vastly more powerful than any river, and the intense actions of currents, tides, and especially waves offered immense challenges. Of course, such rafting had been tried many times over thousands of years. Theophrastus, a Greek philosopher and botanist writing in the third century BCE, tells of the Romans importing lumber from Corsica on giant rafts with up to fifty sails. Yet this route was fairly short, considerably less than two hundred miles, and in relatively safe waters. Even so, one wonders as well if Theophrastus' tale might be apocryphal, or at least hugely exaggerated: it is hard to imagine such a vessel, built with the technology available in that era, not breaking up in the open sea.

In 1791 a lumberman named James Tupper tried to take a raft of timber from Maine to England, but it was not successful: it "barely got out of the harbor." Alice Benson Allen notes this failure only proved that "no raft laden with several million board feet of lumber could withstand the pounding of the open sea." A more "modern" attempt to build a seagoing log raft came in the 1880s when Captain H.R. Robertson built a raft to bring logs from New Brunswick, Canada, to Boston and New York. While the raft worked, it was so ponderous that even launching it was a long and tedious process. Apparently, the captain of the tug that was bringing this raft to New York cut the tow line for reasons that are unclear today; the raft was never seen again. Others on the East Coast also attempted to use rafts at this time, especially St. John, New Brunswick, contractor

James D. Leary. These rafts had extremely limited success in bringing large quantities of timber to the hungry markets of New York. *The New York Times* reported on the arrival of a raft containing 3.5 million board feet in 1891. It also noted the arrival of an even larger raft of 4.5 million board feet in 1907. But these were the exceptions: raging storms in the North Atlantic destroyed others, including one of the first and largest. It was launched in September 1888 in the Bay of Fundy but was soon destroyed by "a terrific equinoxial storm [sic]." In the wake of that incident, says *The American Architect and Building News* in 1907, "shipmasters have reported sighting units of the raft in various parts of the North Atlantic as far north as Greenland."

Robertson also attempted to build rafts for the West Coast. One of his large rafts was lost at sea in 1900, either to accident or, possibly, sabotage: the tow line appeared to have been cut, and there were some suspicions about the captain of the vessel that found the raft and claimed salvage rights, though nothing was definitively proved. There were as well attempts by Robertson to build seagoing rafts at Coos Bay, Oregon, and at Stella on the Washington side of the Columbia. These rafts suffered high losses due to insufficient structural integrity and the builders "had not used the right system of chaining the rafts." Benson knew he had to come up with many significant improvements.

Benson now turned to a man whom he had taken on as a partner a few years before, O.J. Evenson. As we have seen, Benson had already turned over much of the management of Benson Logging and Lumber to his oldest son Amos. Evenson apparently came into full partnership with Benson sometime around the turn of the twentieth century. He may have taken on the role of overseeing the mill operations, or he might have joined William Kidney or taken over his role of supervising day-to-day operations in the lumber camps, while Amos oversaw the front-office management side from the company's headquarters in Clatskanie, where he also had a fine house, as his father spent more and more time at his home in Portland. Amos did well: one writer says, "He was an apt pupil, readily mastering every phase of the business, and he modernized and perfected in every way the methods of handling lumber and doubled the output of the plant. He perfected a very efficient organization, controlling the operations of the mills and camps, while his father remained the executive head of the business, with offices in Portland."

SIMON BENSON

Ole Johan Evenson was born in 1868 in St. Croix County, Wisconsin, not terribly far from where Benson had started his life in the logging business at Black River Falls. His father, W.T. Evenson, had immigrated to the United States from Norway and had been a successful builder and operator of sawmills. His mother, Esther Lythson, also a Norwegian immigrant, had the terrifying experience of seeing her father and mother both die of cholera as they were arriving in Wisconsin, leaving her at 14 in charge of her three younger siblings. She and W.T. Evenson went on to have ten children of their own; she and their eight sons all eventually relocated to Oregon and Washington. O.J. Evenson received a more thorough formal education than Benson, graduating from River Falls Academy at the age of 17, but he lacked Benson's years of practical experience. Also, he did not have the firsthand experience of both felling and moving extremely large trees that Benson had. Evenson followed his father by working in sawmills; he came to Oregon like so many others for the

*O.J. Evenson.
(Photo courtesy of
James Aalberg)*

promise of better timber harvests. He arrived in Portland in 1900 and must have caught Benson's attention quickly since by 1906 he clearly held a senior position in the Benson Logging and Lumber organization.

Benson worked with Evenson to develop a new kind of oceangoing raft. Histories of this period disagree on whether the main contribution to the result came from Benson or Evenson – Ralph Andrews, influenced perhaps by O.J. Evenson's son, in particular appears to believe Evenson deserves most of the credit – but it seems fair to say that the two men's skills and backgrounds would give them a more or less equal and perhaps even complementary ability to come up with the resulting rafts. At any rate, Evenson was apparently happy enough to give Benson the credit for them, as did others involved in the project, and to this day they are remembered as "Benson rafts." Benson himself said, "If you want the job done right, do it yourself."

The design they came up with resembled a cigar – a "perfecto" cigar, fatter in the center and narrowing at both ends, not a panatela or other "straight" cigar type. The rafts that were built by Robertson at Stella, Washington, were comparable, but more cylindrical in shape and not as strong. Benson and Evenson knew a key to building a successful oceangoing raft would be to predict and allow for the natural movement of the vessel as it ran through the constant pushing, pulling, pounding, and twisting that would come from the rough ocean waters, far stronger,

J.A. Fastabend. (Photo courtesy of James Aalberg)

more constant, and more intense than any river. One innovation they came up with was to make the whole raft "self-tightening": once the raft was completed and floating free it would start to flatten out somewhat, and this combined with the movement of the raft through the water would cause the chains circling it to tighten.

To help them with their design efforts, Benson and Evenson hired John Antone Fastabend, an engineer from Astoria, Oregon, to supervise construction. (Some historical sources say the name was spelled "Festabend," but the spelling used here is the one more frequently found.) Fastabend was born in 1853 in Padberg,

SIMON BENSON

Westphalia, Prussia. His family arrived in America in 1869. He came to Astoria from Salt Lake City to supervise building and bridge construction for a proposed railroad linking Astoria with Hillsboro, about fifteen miles west of Portland. When the first transcontinental railroad link arrived in Portland to join it with the rest of the country in 1883, Astorians expected it to continue to their significant port. However, the Northern Pacific chose to stop at Goble, not far beyond Portland, and build a ferry to haul trains across to Kalama, Washington, to carry on to Seattle. At the time the resulting steamboat *Kalama*, built to carry rail cars and locomotives, was the second-largest ferry in the world. Astoria was left out, which caused a good deal of civic resentment along with several plans for railroad construction that were proposed in the late 1880s and early '90s.

    Fastabend apparently led some construction work at Smith's Point in Astoria as part of the railroad project, but this project, like several other planned efforts, came to nothing, and the company behind the project went under in the Depression of 1893. He was available when Benson came looking for a construction manager for his rafts, and Fastabend had already worked with some success on designing smaller rafts for H.R. Robertson at Stella.

Benson and Evenson got in touch with Fastabend and bought the patents for the Robertson rafts, then set out to improve on them.

They chose to build the rafts at Wallace Slough near Clatskanie, close to Benson's timber operations. The dictionary defines a *slough*, in American English pronounced "sloo," as a swampy area or just muddy ground. Several sloughs are located in the Clatskanie area, but not all meet the dictionary's definition. Beaver Slough was wide enough and deep enough for Benson to build his Clatskanie mill on its banks, which meant logs could be rafted right up to it. Technically, Wallace Slough is not really a slough at all: it is simply a fairly narrow channel between the Oregon bank of the Columbia River and Wallace Island. But it was plenty large enough to build giant rafts and get them out conveniently. It might have been easier to float the logs to Astoria and build the rafts closer to the Pacific Ocean, but the plan was to build the rafts during winter then let them wait until summer to tow them down the coast. This meant they would spend considerable time sitting in the water and in this case, Astoria was too close to the ocean's saltwater which could come well up the river with the rising tide. The problem was "borers" such as gribbles, mollusks of the genus

Limnoria the size of fleas that attack wood submerged in seawater. This is why owners of wooden docks and pilings must coat the wood with creosote and other preservatives or see it destroyed. Because the Benson rafts consisted of untreated wood, they could only be exposed to saltwater for a minimal time and had to be kept in fresh river water for as long as possible; the wooden "cradle" in which the rafts were put together also required protection from the borers. Benson and Evenson settled on a building site that was located well away from the saltwater as well as close to the forests whence the logs originally came, near Benson's properties. Much of the timber was brought to the site in flat river rafts; it took about twenty-four river rafts to build a single ocean-going raft. Railroad tracks were also laid to allow trains to bring the timber to the edge of the slough.

Aerial view of raft construction, 1917. (Photo courtesy of James Aalberg)

The first step was for Fastabend to oversee the building of the cradle to hold the raft during construction. The cradle, or form, floated in the slough and was built in sections held together by an "interlocking device"; it floated high in the water when empty and rather resembled the ribs of a wooden sailing ship under construction. Stewart Holbrook says it looked "like the ribs of some monster of the days of dinosaurs." One side of the cradle remained tied to pilings beside the riverbank while the other could be removed when the time came to "kick out" the finished raft and haul it into the river. A floating crane with a one-hundred-foot boom picked up logs from the slough and placed them in the frame. One factor behind the rafts' success was their sturdiness. This came in part from the use of as many extra-long logs as possible. Most were "tree-length": between fifty and 150 feet long. As Holbrook says, the big logs would offer "a necessary lap and backbone to resist the action of waves and ground swells." "[T]hey could withstand the assault of other huge logs placed on top during the building operation." These logs could be extremely heavy, so an extra-powerful derrick was needed to lift them out of the water. Lacking the support and traction the ground would normally provide, the floating derrick would sometimes tip almost all the way over from the weight of a huge log.

Laying logs into the cradle to form a raft.
(Wikipedia photo)

In *Holy Old Mackinaw*, his wonderful history of logging in America, Holbrook vividly describes the construction process, which he saw firsthand. Outside the cradle, he says,

> a floating derrick moves back and forth, meanwhile lifting, pulling, pushing, and dropping logs this way and that – pickin' 'em up and layin' 'em down, the raft boys call it. It is a job for specialists, because although every size and length of log is used, the strength of the entire raft depends on there being a

large portion of tree-length material in its make-up....

The derrick working looks like a gigantic game of jackstraws, in reverse, for the process is a threading together rather than of disentangling. The big machine, snorting and puffing, picks up the huge sticks as though they were matches, placing them exactly where the foreman wants them.

Putting a raft together. (Wikipedia photo)

During construction, workers installed a large two-and-one-half-inch anchor chain along the raft's centerline. More chains were then attached to the center chain and circle chains at each end of the raft. A spare tow chain attached to one of the circling chains near the end of the raft provided a backup in the event of an emergency. This construction technique, along with the raft's cigar shape, also made it possible to tow the raft from either end, making it easier to maneuver. The circling chains were placed about every fifteen to twenty feet, and still more chains attached the circling chains to each other. Each raft would carry from 175 tons up to 250 tons of chains alone, each one carefully placed and tightened. This construction made the rafts both reasonably flexible and incredibly strong, able to withstand the power of the ocean. "One chain not in place," says Holbrook, "and the raft would never stand the pounding it will get on its voyage of more than a thousand miles."

Close-up photo of raft showing chains that would hold it together. (Photo courtesy of the Oregon Historical Society)

*"Kicking out" a raft, setting it free from the cradle.
(Photo courtesy of James Aalberg)*

Benson would have the rafts built during the winter months, then let them sit waiting in holding ponds until the better weather of summer allowed the tugs to take them south. Sometimes there would be three or four rafts waiting their turn in the holding ponds. Each raft took about six weeks to build. The cradle would sink as the raft grew in size until it was largely or even entirely under water. The cradle was 960 feet long, but the ends of the raft would stick out at either end. Benson's first, experimental raft was "only" about six to seven hundred feet long, but most of the subsequent ones measured approximately one thousand feet long; the comparison to Leviathan was a favorite bit of imagery among contemporary observers. Holbrook tells a story about one witness:

> Nobody believed the fisherman that day in 1906 when he came charging wild-eyed into the sailors' retreat shouting that he had seen a whale longer than a freight train chasing a boat down the Columbia River. He'd been fishing nearby, along the banks of the Columbia a short way above Astoria, minding his own business too. Almost hysterical, he sobbed out his story.
>
> He'd heard this wallowing noise like a huge animal thrashing in the water, and when he looked up, there was a whale all right. "He's a thousand feet long," he shouted, "and chasing a tugboat. You can still see it toward the mouth of the river."
>
> Above the shouting a voice said, "Hell, that's an ocean-going raft old man Benson's been building up at Wallace Slough. They're towing her to San Diego."

Each raft's width would average about fifty feet, and about thirty-five feet height, of which up to twenty-eight feet would be underwater. They required about thirty feet of water to launch. When the raft was finished the outer portion of the cradle was removed and the raft would be kicked out sideways into the slough. Special towing lamps that could burn continuously for thirty days – impressive new technology in that era – were the final touch in the construction process. In some years, several rafts would be built during autumn, winter, and spring, then would wait outside the main channel of the Columbia for the optimal towing season, which lasted from about 15 June to 15 September.

    A typical one-thousand-foot raft would carry up to six million board feet of timber and would cover more than an acre. At the time, a Benson raft was "the largest thing afloat in the Pacific"; it would contain enough timber to build several hundred houses: "…five million feet of boards, and such, is enough to build two hundred fifty good-sized homes. Say about the five-room type." The only thing that can compare in size even now is a modern American aircraft carrier. In addition to the raw logs, most of the rafts carried other cargo. After the raft could float free from the cradle it would flatten out somewhat,

Raft and tug while still on the Columbia River. (Photo courtesy of the Oregon Historical Society)

allowing workers to stack large amounts of finished lumber products on top. At least half the rafts carried "deck loads" consisting of items such as shingles, spars, telephone poles, and fence posts.

SIMON BENSON

River tugs of the Portland-based Shaver Transportation Company towed the rafts as far as Astoria. Three sternwheeler tugs would guide each raft downriver, one at the bow and two at the stern. At Astoria, an oceangoing tug took over and began the long trip to San Diego. Crowley Launch and Tugboat Company (now known as Crowley Maritime) vessels from the San Francisco Bay Area, with their distinctive red stacks, pulled most of the rafts over the years, though another company may have taken the first loads. The trip was long and grueling: with such a large load, the tugs could only average between sixty and seventy miles a day at a speed of perhaps three knots. The entire 1,080-mile trip took about two weeks. Towing each raft cost eight to ten thousand dollars. Lloyd's of London insured the rafts.

The first raft was towed by the tug *Dauntless*, commanded by Capt. J.W. Darragh. She left Astoria on 24 August 1906 and arrived in San Diego on 7 September. One writer says this raft carried the necessary lumber to build "a complete Benson sawmill" in San Diego. He appears to have got this from W.T. Evenson, one of O.J. Evenson's sons, who wrote:

> The first raft was small compared to [later ones]…and contained not only piling and sawlogs of all shapes and sizes, but several hundred thousand feet of sawn timbers and lumber for a complete sawmill to be erected in San Diego….The information on this trip resulted in several improvements. The first raft arrived in perfect condition, and construction started on the mill as soon as the raft could be opened up.

However, others say the mill had already been built in anticipation of the rafts, and this seems more probable. Benson had added milling to the incorporation of the Benson Logging and Lumber Company and had also already bought sixteen acres of waterfront property in San Diego; it seems likely he would have wanted the mill ready when the first raft arrived. Milling his own wood was an integral part of Benson's business plan. He wanted to control the entire process of creating lumber, from beginning to end. His company would cut down the trees, bring the timber to the mills, and turn it into lumber ready for market – all in a huge market hungry for wood and ready to pay top dollar for it. Benson loved making money and hated letting someone else make it when he could do so himself and reap all the profit.

The first raft arrives in San Diego. (Photo courtesy of the San Diego History Center)

Witnesses to the first raft's arrival expressed astonishment equal to that of the stunned Astoria fisherman, but their excitement was mixed with joy. "Prolonged blasts from nearly all the steam whistles in town heralded the arrival of the big Benson log raft at noon today during its slow passage up the bay [and] crowds of people hastened to the waterfront. Before the big mass of timber had reached the wharves all the docks were lined with spectators," said the San Diego *Union-Tribune.* The raft arrived in perfect condition; the only casualty of the trip was the telephone cable connecting San Diego and Coronado. The raft had run it over and severed it. The raft's arrival was seen as a significant occasion. "[T]he raft was secured at the foot of Sigsbee Street," says historian Jerry MacMullen of the Serra Museum in San Diego, and then

> [w]ithin an hour the raft was swarming with people, none of whom had any idea of stumbling clumsily over a log-butt, breaking two or three legs, and then suing somebody. Decorations were provided, the City Guard band was tootling its sweetest melodies, and before you could say "Avast heaving!" people were making flowery speeches. A little girl was selected to break a bottle of champagne over the biggest log, and why the W.C.T.U. didn't make an issue of that phase of the party is anyone's guess.

Some came aboard the rafts even sooner. O.J. Evenson accompanied the first raft to San Diego, and he told his son Franklin, "Boaters would meet the raft at Point Loma, board it, and ride the thing to the lumber company's docking place."

Rafts awaiting breaking-up in San Diego. (Photo courtesy of James Aalberg)

Some of the first raft's timber served an unanticipated purpose. Rather than being milled for commercial lumber it was taken to the Imperial Valley east of San Diego. On 9 August 1906 the Colorado River spilled some three hundred million cubic feet of water per hour through a "ruptured irrigation intake." (One cubic foot of water comprises about seven and one-half gallons.) Multiple efforts to close the intake failed, and engineers were at a loss. Finally, an engineer named Harry Thomas Cory advanced a revolutionary plan to bring the river back under control. This involved dumping hundreds of tons of rock in the path of the river and using large amounts of wood to shore up the rock and build trestles for trains to reach the work sites. The first raft arrived in San Diego at exactly the right moment, and much of its wood went by train straight to the flooded area.

Over the ensuing thirty-five years, one hundred twenty rafts would make the trip south, typically between two and six per year. Only four were lost, two to storms and two, apparently, to fire. However, Benson could boast that he personally had "never lost a raft" because the losses all came after he sold his holdings in the lumber business. Despite this sale he continued to make money because he and Evenson had patented the rafts and so made money off each voyage. Although the rafts sailed only during the nicer, calmer weather of the summer months, storms remained a potential danger, but the rafts were built to handle rough seas. "If we hit rough weather when I was shipping the rafts," Benson said, "the steamer cast loose and stood by and let the raft wallow in the trough of the sea till the storm blew itself out. Then we re-attached the cable to the raft and went on." An occasional log might break free of the raft and be lost, but this was rare. Because the rafts were so huge, towing them could be a challenge, and captains sometimes said it was difficult to tell if their tug was pulling the raft or vice versa. Writing in the 1910s,

> SAN DIEGO CITY DIRECTORY. 65
> **LUMBER MANUFACTURERS AND DEALERS**
>
> Frank Lynch, Pres.   Phones—Main 18, Home 3367   O. J. Evenson, Secy.
> F. M. White, Genl. Manager.   E. E.Coovert, Vice-Pres.
>
> ## FREE "A Sight Worth Seeing" FREE
>
> Visit The Monster Ocean Going
>
> # LOG RAFTS
>
> Containing over 4,000,000 feet of logs in a raft.
> Rafts over 600 feet long.
>
> # BENSON LUMBER CO.
> Foot Sigsbee St. and Bay Front
> Dealers in "Everything in Lumber from a Raft to a Rafter."

*Advertisement in the San Diego City Directory.
(Photo courtesy of Renato Rodriguez)*

when nearly thirty rafts had successfully made the long journey, Fastabend himself described Benson's design as "about perfect." He too was apparently happy enough to give Benson primary credit for the rafts' design, though Fastabend himself also deserves considerable credit for the engineering.

As the supply of trees near Wallace Slough started to dwindle in the 1930s, the building operation was moved across the river to a site near Cathlamet, Washington. Logs could be brought here from the still-profitable Deep River operation.

*Building a later raft near Cathlamet, Washington.
(Photo courtesy of James Aalberg)*

*

One of the most hard-working of the tugs that towed the rafts was the *Hercules*. She hauled many of the rafts over the years, starting soon after her construction in 1908. Today she still stands berthed, a museum piece now, part of the collection of the San Francisco Maritime National Historical Park. She rarely leaves the dock these days, but the park staff still keep her in good running order, and visitors can see how powerful she is. The tug has an overall length of more than one hundred feet and its wheelhouse stands some three stories above the water line; good visibility would have been essential on the kinds of cruises the *Hercules* made. Her steam engine could generate one thousand horsepower or more, and she is said to hold the all-time record for the heaviest load ever hauled by a steam vessel; not surprisingly, this was one of the Benson rafts.

Tug Hercules, *now docked at the San Francisco Maritime National Historical Park. (Photo by author)*

The long, slow voyages from Astoria to San Diego appear to have been hard on the crew, largely due to their frustration and boredom. Each trip took two weeks or more, at an agonizingly slow pace of about two knots. Sailors told stories of going on watch and seeing a lighthouse or headland on shore, and when their watch ended four hours later, it would still be there; the sailors would feel they had hardly moved at all. The boredom extended to food as well: fresh meat and vegetables would not last long without refrigeration, and to stop to replenish supplies would mean losing money. So,

The Hercules *bringing a raft into port. (Photo courtesy of the San Francisco Maritime National Historical Park)*

the crew had to make do with canned or salted foods. Occasionally an off-duty crewman would catch a fish, which was always a moment for celebration. Arrival in San Diego must have led to much liquid celebration, followed by relief as the *Hercules* made her way home to San Francisco at a more reasonable rate of speed.

The rafts may be perceived as a boon for all parties involved. Benson's gamble paid off and he made plenty of money from the project, as did his partners. San Diegans correctly saw in the rafts a promising new source of income as well as badly needed building supplies for the growing region. Even today, the occasional article on San Diego's history will appear locally, describing how the rafts "helped Oregon build San Diego." In 1925, G.H. Woodward, the cashier for the Benson Lumber Company (the name remained long after Benson sold his interest in the operation), said that the sixty-seven rafts that had sailed up to that time had carried some 335 million board feet of timber, enough wood to build thirty-seven thousand six-room houses. In the early 1920s, well after Benson had retired from the business, O.J. Evenson apparently seriously considered the possibility of taking rafts to Japan. At the time Asia in general and Japan in particular had become major consumers of Northwest timber. In March of

1922, more than thirty-two million feet of lumber was exported overseas by traditional shipping methods from Oregon and Washington; two-thirds of it went to Asia, mostly to Japan. For some time, the Japanese had expressed interest in trans-Pacific rafting, and Evenson apparently had lengthy discussions with G. Shikimura of Akita Mokusari Kaisha, a prominent Japanese lumber firm. Evenson told Shikimura that such a venture would be extremely risky. A trans-Pacific raft would need up to eighty days to make the crossing and a tug with eighteen hundred horsepower and considerable fuel-storage capacity would be required to handle the crossing. However, he also said he thought the trip could be made safely during July and August when few storms hit the northern Pacific. The proposed plan apparently came to nothing, although Japan remained a significant trading partner of the Northwest until World War II ended all trade activities between the Japan and the United States. Understanding the strategic importance of the Northwest timber, the Japanese actually experimented with destroying it with incendiary bombs during the war. On 9 September 1942, a plane launched from a submarine dropped two bombs in the forest near Brookings on the southern Oregon coast. The effort caused no significant damage other than to leave the pilot terrified. Later in the war, the Japanese also experimented with sending bombs over the American West suspended from unmanned balloons, following the newly discovered jet stream, with the express purpose of starting forest fires. A party of several civilian picnickers was killed near Bly, Oregon, in 1945. The Japanese sought to undermine the American economy as a whole as well as hinder its war effort. They understood that wood was a vital commodity and destroying the forests would harm the economy intensely. Fortunately, the lacked the technology to cause damage on a sufficiently large scale.

Benson had already started to distance himself from day-to-day operations of his companies well before the raft project began. As we have seen, his son Amos and O.J. Evenson were handling the company activities in Clatskanie, and he also engaged Frank Lynch to run the mill in San Diego. Lynch would eventually buy out the San Diego operation from Benson and also take over the rafting operations. In August 1941 the last raft sailed out of the Columbia, but off Monterey, California, it caught fire and was destroyed. How a raft floating in the ocean could burn so thoroughly has never been clear, but Lynch suspected sabotage both in this case and in a previous raft fire the year before. America's direct involvement in the war had not yet started but tensions with Japan were high and only a few months later the attack on Pearl Harbor would take place. Citing rising insurance costs as well as fear of more sabotage, Lynch ended the rafting program.

The mill employed up to one hundred sixty people and could process up to two million feet of lumber per month. Supposedly, construction in Southern California doubled within four years after the arrival of Benson's lumber. Changing times caused Lynch to shut down the mill in 1946; workers dropped its last vestige, an eighty-foot chimney, in May of 1957. San Diego's 10th Avenue Pier now occupies the mill site.

One of the great themes of Benson's life is looking to the future. When he first decided to come west in 1879, he based his decision on the belief that logging in the upper Midwest would not last much longer, and that the future of the industry lay in the Northwest. In the early 1890s he saw that technology would revolutionize logging, and despite his lack of formal education he was surely "one of history's most gifted amateur engineers." He was confident he could adapt the new technology to his needs, and he succeeded in doing so with railroads and steam power. In the early years of the twentieth century, he recognized that a significant aspect of the nation's and the economy's future lay in Southern California, and if he could adapt technology again, he could ride that wave to financial success as well as fame and honor. This theme of seeing things to come and wanting to be part of them would continue into the next important phase of Benson's life.

    The rafts were a huge success for Benson, who had found a way to control his shipping costs and not feel beholden to other companies. He took a major gamble, investing many thousands of dollars in the project, but it paid off wonderfully. As he put it, "I had found the solution to low freights. I built a big mill at San Diego and shipped twelve rafts of logs, saving two dollars a thousand on freight, thus making an extra profit of a hundred and fifty thousand dollars." The rafts would make Benson very wealthy indeed, as would his sale of the by now highly lucrative logging and milling operations. They would also mark the beginning of the end of his participation in those industries. His interests would turn to other pursuits.

SIMON BENSON

*Aerial view of Benson rafts and mill in San Diego.
(Photo courtesy of James Aalberg)*

Chapter 5: New Perspectives, New Interests

During the first decade of the twentieth century, Benson began to find interests beyond logging, milling, and the related activities in which he had been involved. In 1909, he began selling his holdings around Clatskanie, starting with a sale of twenty-seven thousand acres to the Fir Tree Lumber Company. In 1911, he sold the final fifteen thousand acres he owned to O.J. Evenson, Frank Lynch, and another partner for something more than two million dollars. This would translate to well over fifty million dollars today. For a while they continued to run it as the Benson Timber Company; later they changed it to the Benson-Evenson Timber Company. O.J. Evenson died in 1938, but the company still operates today, now only under the name of Evenson, with O.J.'s descendants still operating it. The sale included eight hundred million feet of fir and a twelve-mile logging railroad.

SIMON BENSON

Frank Lynch bought the San Diego mill holdings in 1911 as well; these consisted of "a planing mill, sash and door factory, and a wharf that jutted four hundred and fifty feet into the bay." The mill could handle five hundred thousand feet of lumber per day. In describing the sale, Benson noted he had made four hundred thousand dollars in profits on the mill in about four years, and that was the price he asked Lynch to pay for it, but Lynch only had fifty thousand immediately available. "I told him he could have the mill out of the profits," Benson said. "From the profits he was able to pay the other three hundred and fifty thousand in three years." Lynch continued to operate the business under the name Benson Lumber Company. As we have seen, in August of 1941, a raft mysteriously burned; fearing sabotage by Japanese agents as tensions built toward war, Lynch closed the rafting operation due to rising insurance costs. He closed the mill after World War II.

Frank Lynch. (Photo courtesy of James Aalberg)

Benson's move to Portland at the turn of the century had reminded him that there was a world beyond just logging and lumber. He had begun to take an interest in other things, including fun and travel with his family. Amos had become a member of the family business, but he was also already grown up and married, and he had married again after his first wife died. He had been living his own life in his own home for several years. Alice, however, offers a number of happy memories of living in her father's household and shows him at play with her and Caroline. These included many trips to California, notably to Palm Springs and the San Jacinto Mountains; to Del Monte, Paso Robles, Santa Barbara; to Pasadena to see the Tournament of Roses Parade and what might have been the very first Rose Bowl football game; to Long Beach to stay at the opulent Virginia Hotel.

One particularly memorable visit came in the spring of 1906, when Benson took Alice to San Francisco to see Caroline, who was attending Stanford University in nearby Palo Alto. They stayed in the St. Francis Hotel and attended the opera, where they heard the famous Italian tenor Enrico Caruso sing. Early the next morning they were awakened by "violent shaking of the hotel and sounds of confusion outside." It was, of course, the great San Francisco earthquake of 1906, which struck shortly after five a.m. on 18 April. Father and daughter made their way to Palo Alto, where they found Caroline's sorority house considerably damaged and Caroline herself suffering from minor injuries. They brought her home to Portland to recover, and soon after, Benson took his daughters to Honolulu, Hawaii, "as a special treat after the disaster." They stayed at the Moana Hotel, coincidentally, in the suite that had belonged to Mrs. Leland Stanford, who with her husband had founded the university.

Alice always described her father in glowing terms; her book about him reads like a hagiography – the biography of a saint. She does not always provide reliable information in the book, but some of the most enjoyable and interesting portions are her firsthand descriptions of life with him. She describes him as a "prolific reader of history, politics, finance, and labor," and he thought the United States might someday have a "labor president." One wonders what he might have thought of some of the American presidents who came after his death. As he was deeply conservative and pro-business, one suspects he would have loved Eisenhower and Reagan. He also enjoyed pinochle and other card games, but he was not much fun to play with because he would quickly memorize every card. He was a good athlete and enjoyed lawn bowling. He may have retained a slight Norwegian accent, but he had a completely fluent command of both spoken and written English.

*

Benson also began to show signs suggesting he was interested in gaining recognition beyond the forest. Perhaps the first hint of this came in April of 1899, when he offered for public inspection the "first all-steam logging show in the Northwest." He opened his Oak Point operation to the public and newspaper reporters to show off his exciting, high-tech operations. A favorite attraction was seeing the enormous fir logs sent down the thousand-foot chute to the Columbia River, into which they would splash in spectacular fashion. Benson also gained some publicity soon after when he provided a spectacular 150-foot "stick of timber" that was presented to Japan for its national flagpole in Yokohama. Benson proudly stated that an even longer, more perfect "stick" could "readily have been found."

At this time, Benson was developing a reputation as the best operator providing the best timber in the Northwest. He was proud to show off that he could not only produce logs in large quantities, but he could also provide timber of the best size and quality. His daughter says he had by now "an international reputation for quality timber." He was, she says, able to charge well above the typical market prices of the day: as much as ten to twelve dollars per board foot when the going rate was closer to two dollars. (Timber prices could be volatile. There is newspaper coverage of a meeting of timber operators in Oregon and Washington to extend the usual July Fourth holiday to a month-long closure in the hope it would drive depressed prices up. The effort failed when Benson and Weyerhaeuser, among others, refused to go along.)

*

Benson worked to support and build his reputation. An excellent opportunity to do this, one that would directly influence his future, came in 1904, with an invitation to help create one of the premier exhibits at the 1905 Lewis and Clark Centennial Exposition in Portland. This was the era of great world's fairs: every city with pretensions of international importance hosted one. Such fairs can be dated back as far as the 1790s, but the first truly memorable one would have to be the Great Exhibition of London in 1851. This became something of a model for future expositions in many cities. Various nations and, in America, individual cities and states offered exhibitions and pavilions, as did industries and large companies. Subsequent notable fairs included the 1889 Exposition Universelle in Paris, for which the Eiffel Tower was built; the 1893 World's Columbian Exposition in Chicago, celebrating the four-hundredth anniversary of the arrival of Christopher Columbus to North America (a year late due to delays); the 1901 Pan-American Exposition in Buffalo, New York, at which President William McKinley was assassinated; the 1904 Louisiana Purchase Exposition in St. Louis, Missouri, which introduced the ice cream cone; and, as we will see later, the Panama-Pacific International Exposition in San Francisco. Other famous later expositions include the 1939 and 1964 World's Fairs in New York City, and the 1962 Century 21 Exposition in Seattle, Washington, which introduced the Space Needle. Cities around the world continue to offer fairs and expositions, though they lack the grandiosity and excitement of those in years past.

The year 1905 marked the centennial of the Lewis and Clark Expedition, celebrating the two famed explorers who led a team – the Corps of Discovery – across the portion of North America recently acquired in the Louisiana Purchase, all the way to the Pacific Ocean. The expedition was a great success, with few serious casualties and mostly good relations with the Native Americans the explorers encountered along the way. Lewis and Clark and their team spent the winter of 1805-06 in a structure they built near Astoria, Oregon, called Fort Clatsop. A rather good replica of it still stands today. The explorers actually hated the location, and perhaps the entire Northwest coastal region, where it rained on all but two days during the several winter months they spent there, and where they subsisted mostly on elk and salmon; salmon at that time was not considered the delicacy it is today. Lewis and the other expedition members missed a delicacy they had discovered during the journey: dog meat. However, Clark would not touch it. All in all, the Corps of Discovery found the fort at Astoria so unpleasant, they left sooner than they should have, before the snow had fully melted in the mountains, but they just could not bear to stay any longer.

In spite of this reality, the people of Oregon and especially Portland adopted Lewis and Clark as their great symbol of the opening of the American West. In the early twentieth century, "boosterism" became all the rage as cities sought to bring in people and investment. To bring attention to Portland, nothing would do but to offer a fine international exposition to celebrate the centennial of the expedition; its official title was the Lewis and Clark

Centennial and American Pacific Exposition and Oriental Fair – this was also an era of giving grandiose names. In this case, the title intended to remind people how close Portland lay to the great markets of Asia. America's imperialist expansion had recently added Hawaii and the Philippines to the nation's sphere of influence. Business leaders in Portland also knew that thanks to the railroad network that now joined all the nation's important cities, large numbers of visitors could be expected. "Visitors would spend money on train tickets, hotel rooms, food, and drink," says Carl Abbott in an article on the fair in *The Oregon Encyclopedia*, "and the Northern Pacific Railroad and brewer Henry Weinhard were among the biggest financial backers." In 1903, the Oregon legislature granted four hundred fifty thousand dollars to choose a site and build a number of exhibits; the federal government provided several times more money. A site of some four hundred acres was selected at Guild's Lake, near the northwest edge of Portland. Jon Charles Olmsted, nephew and adopted son of the famed landscape architect Frederick Law Olmsted who planned Central Park in New York City, designed the grounds. The park plan he laid out was such a thoughtful complement to the city, it still "resonates more than a century later." Logging being one of the primary industries of Oregon and the Northwest at the time, the timber and lumber companies wanted to have a significant presence. The fair planners chose to build what would be even to this day the world's all-time largest log cabin, to be known as the Forestry Building, and they asked Simon Benson to provide most of the timber. Benson signed a contract in February 1904 for a large quantity of "sound live timber with bark in perfect condition," to be cut "before the sap runs." It was to be delivered by rail or raft, depending on whether it was cut in Oregon or Washington. In the event, the logs were chosen from the Oak Point, Washington, camp, each carefully selected for both beauty and uniformity of size and shape. They were transported by train, one log to a car, to the Columbia River, then taken in two rafts to Clatskanie where they waited until the Willamette River reached high enough water at the fair site.

SIMON BENSON

The Forestry Building at the Lewis and Clark Exposition, the largest log cabin in the world, built with lumber supplied by Benson. (Wikipedia photo)

The Forestry Building celebrated the "Glory Days of Logging" and the region's "magnificent virgin forests." The building had a portico of tree trunks and measured 209 feet by 105 feet. It stood seventy-two feet tall. Inside, fifty-two log columns, each six feet wide, supported the roof and a smaller upstairs gallery. It was truly an impressive sight. Even today the building appears spectacular in photographs. Its interior looked something like the nave of

Forestry Building interior. (Wikipedia photo)

a church, with displays of wildlife as well as logging and lumber operations; photos of Native Americans decorated the walls. Sections of even larger logs, as much as ten feet in diameter, were displayed on the floor, along with "polished slabs of many kinds of commercial lumber." The logs if placed end to end would have stretched some two miles, and each of the large logs contained enough lumber to build "several houses." It was a "veritable cathedral of giant trees."

In today's era of conservation and environmental awareness, one cannot help but be struck by these descriptions of huge logs in seemingly limitless quantity. With the disappearance of almost all of the old-growth timber, most readers nowadays will have to look at photographs or use their imaginations to picture logs so huge, a single one could form the entire load of a logging truck. On his company's letterhead, Benson included a picture of a log being pulled by a train. It was so long, it had to ride on a specially designed rail system that included a small car at each end, with the log hanging free in the middle. Today's logging companies publicly proclaim that they have become more environmentally responsible and carefully plant new trees of fast-growing varieties, making their industry much more efficient and renewable. They see themselves as harvesting crops that will come back in a few years. But we will likely never again see those spectacular giants of the past.

The Forestry Building was one of the highlights of the exposition. Visitors to the fair loved it: it was the only building from the exposition not torn down when the fair was closed and the fairground became what is now the Guild's Lake industrial area of northwest Portland. The Forestry Building remained a popular and famous tourist attraction for some fifty-nine years; supposedly the City of New York sought to buy it at one point but was turned away disappointed. Ultimately, it was destroyed by fire in 1964. It also became the direct forerunner of the World

SIMON BENSON

Forestry Center located today in Portland's West Hills near the Oregon Zoo.

*

It seems reasonable to say that Benson's move to Portland at the turn of the century offered him a new perspective on life. Heretofore, Benson had spent most of his time living in small settlements like Oak Point, or in the logging camps with his crews, where he would have focused almost exclusively on business. The largest town where he had spent an appreciable amount of time was Colfax; that was years before, and for the most part he had only lived there part-time. He would only visit significantly large cities on business. Now, however, things had changed. Son Amos was now in charge of running the day-to-day operations of Benson Logging and Lumber — it was he who made the decision not to shut down during July 1904 in the hope of raising prices — and Benson himself now lived far from the scene, in the fairly good-sized city of Portland. When Benson signed the contract to provide logs for the Forestry Building, for the first time he could see his work in a new light. The raw timber and the finished lumber he had always provided he now could envision not just as utilitarian materials for everyday houses and buildings; it also could be considered as something that provided beauty, fame, and glory to his adopted home – and by extension, himself.

Designing, building, and shipping the great rafts would occupy much of Benson's immediate future in middle of the twentieth century's first decade, but he still found time to enjoy himself in Portland. In 1907, the city celebrated its first Rose Festival, and the following year the Benson family took part by entering a car in the festival's parade. Daughter Alice decorated the family's automobile with flowers, but the car did not win any prizes because she ran out of fresh flowers and substituted artificial ones, violating the parade's rules. However, in 1916, Simon Benson was the parade's Grand Marshal and his car, covered by his own design with huge numbers of pink peonies, won first prize.

The Portland Rose Festival, not to be confused with the Tournament of Roses in California, came directly out of the Lewis and Clark Exposition. At the fair's closing ceremony, Portland Mayor Harry Lane called for a "festival of roses" as a way to celebrate one of Oregon's more beautiful agricultural products and to keep bringing tourists to the region. Portlanders had been proudly hosting rose shows and competitions since the 1880s. The festival continues today, run through a nonprofit organization called the Portland Rose Festival Foundation. The first festival included an "electrical parade," electricity then still being something of a novelty; still today the festival hosts its Starlight Parade. But the crowning event of each year's festival is called the Grand Floral Parade, held a week after the Starlight Parade. It includes enormous and elaborate floats covered top to bottom in fresh flowers, far more inventive than anything imagined by Benson and his children.

As Benson began to enjoy life as a prominent member of the Portland community, and after he had sold off his direct interests in logging and lumber mills, he embarked on an entirely new career…or perhaps it is better to call it a series of projects which gave him a new reputation as a leading businessman in an entirely different field and, more important, as Oregon's foremost philanthropist and benefactor. Throughout the second decade of the twentieth century Benson found several different, unusual, and creative ways to contribute to the adopted community he had come to love. The first of these projects was really the smallest, yet it may have done more than any other to keep Benson's name alive in Portland more than a century later.

*

SIMON BENSON

On 10 April 1912, Benson gave the City of Portland ten thousand dollars with which to install eighteen distinctive, four-bowl drinking fountains. Almost immediately after they first started to appear, Portlanders began calling them "Benson Bubblers," and for many they remain an iconic symbol of Portland. Today as many as fifty-two Bubblers may be found throughout the city and its environs, and a couple have been erected farther afield. In the 1960s as part of a cultural exchange, Portland officials donated a Bubbler to its sister city of Sapporo, Japan; also, Benson's friend Sam Hill, about whom we shall hear much more, asked Benson to have one placed at his glorious Maryhill estate some one hundred miles east of Portland up the Columbia River Gorge. Benson was happy to oblige. The fountains are still quite beautiful today, with a lovely greenish patina that has built up over the years. Occasionally well-meaning citizens attempt to remove the patina but inevitably the result is unsuccessful and looks wrong; the Portland Water Bureau, now in charge of the fountains, always restores the patina

Benson Bubbler.
(Photo by author)

finish in preference to the more gaudy, patina-less copper color.

At least two distinct stories exist explaining the origin of the Bubblers. The more popular one, relayed by Benson's daughter Alice, was that Benson once found himself feeling thirsty on a hot summer day in Portland. Although a teetotaler, he stepped into a saloon hoping to find a drink of water. The bartender rudely said, "Only beer served here!" Benson ordered a beer *and* a glass of water and when they came, he paid his nickel and drank the water and walked out, leaving the beer on the bar. From there he promptly started the project that would result in the Bubblers.

Another version of the story says Benson saw a girl crying at a Fourth of July parade because she was thirsty and could not get a drink of water. Still others say he just wanted to find a way to keep his loggers out of saloons at lunchtime, but since he would be unlikely to find many of his loggers on the streets of Portland, so far from the logging camps, this explanation seems rather improbable. However, Portland had plenty of its own workers using the saloons and bars. Benson said,

SIMON BENSON

> I used to watch the workers going into saloons with their buckets to buy beer. It seemed strange that here in a city whose water is famous for its purity, workmen had no opportunity to quench their thirst except in saloons. I had noticed for years how much liquor had cost me in the decreased efficiency of the men in my logging camps and sawmills. Liquor was also the cause of numerous accidents which were annoying and expensive to me. It also caused poverty and distress in the families of my workmen.... I came to the conclusion that if a workman could get a drink of cold, pure water on a street corner, without any obligation, he probably wouldn't go into a saloon so often.

Benson credited the Bubblers with a great deal of influence: he insisted his gift of the Bubblers "helped knock the profit out of the saloon business and was one of the factors in making Oregon go dry." Benson also claimed to have sent "a responsible agent" on a tour of investigation; he asserted that in many saloons "sales had decreased forty percent." As a strong Prohibitionist and a teetotaler himself, Benson called the fountains "the best investment I ever made."

SIMON BENSON

Simon Benson in front of one of his iconic Benson Bubblers. (Benson family collection)

One wonders how seriously to take this, considering just how popular Prohibition would show alcohol to be, but at any rate, Benson clearly sought to make a significant political statement with the Bubblers. This was the era when the forces calling for Prohibition were at their most powerful. Oregon passed Prohibition laws in 1916, three years before the nation adopted the Volstead Act and the Eighteenth Amendment, and Simon Benson was a firm believer in them. He believed that going dry would "work for better citizenship and it is the quality of our citizenship more than our material resources that makes Oregon a great and worthy state." Despite his views, Benson had been shrewd enough in the past not to force Prohibition on his employees in the camps: according to Stewart Holbrook, in order to avoid having to shut down for up to two weeks during the July Fourth holiday because too many workers became blind drunk, he would bring a barrel of whiskey into the camp a couple of weeks early and let the workers have a lower-key party; they would not feel the need to celebrate so much then during the time when production should have been at its peak. The workers might miss a day or two of work, but they would stay in camp and not miss even more. But while his workers may have been allowed some limited drinking in his camps, in Portland, Benson would do his best to help people adopt his views. So far as is known, Benson also did not smoke, drink, or gamble. He did, however, believe firmly in seeing that his money was well spent for a good return, and he considered the Bubblers an excellent investment. Whether they helped contribute to Oregon adopting Prohibition is a matter for debate, but one must agree that they make a fine legacy. Today the Bubblers are located in various locations throughout downtown Portland.

The Bubblers were designed by Portland architect A. E. Doyle, who was the area's favorite and most widely known architect in the early years of the twentieth century. This was likely not the first time he worked with Benson, but as we will see, it would certainly not be the last.

Albert Ernest Doyle was born in 1877 in California but came to Portland with his family as a young child. He began his architecture career at age 16 as an apprentice to Whidden and Lewis, a leading Portland firm, then spent time in New York City studying architecture at Columbia University. He then returned to Whidden and Lewis in 1904, in time to be involved in planning for the Lewis and Clark Exposition, of which Lewis was the chief architect. Doyle's first big assignment was to design the Forestry Building, for which Benson had provided the logs. While on this occasion Benson

A.E. Doyle. (Photo courtesy of the Oregon Historical Society)

likely would not have had much say in the design, it gave him an opportunity to see the quality of Doyle's work and admire it. In fact, the Forestry Building, one of the few at the fair that was always intended to be a permanent structure, was such a hit that Doyle was able to start his own firm on the strength of it. He would go on to design several Portland structures, many of which are on the National Register of Historic Places. His notable works include the Multnomah County Central Library, the Multnomah Stadium, the U.S. National Bank, the Lipman Wolfe and Meier and Frank department stores, all in Portland, and the Oregon Electric Railway Passenger Station – now a restaurant – in Eugene. His work, especially in the earlier years of his career, shows a definite preference for the classical elements that were popular during the early twentieth century, but later his work started to move in different directions. He died of kidney disease in 1928.

    The Benson Bubblers were an unusual project for an architect like Doyle, but he would play a more traditional role in Benson's next project, one that seemed unusual and out of character for Benson himself. For Benson, the Bubblers may have served as little more than a pleasant gift – albeit with some symbolic sociopolitical overtones – but that next project would mark the beginning of virtually a whole different career. Now at the age of sixty, successful and wealthy beyond anyone's expectations, when most men in his position might be expected to consider retirement, Benson took his first steps on what would prove an entirely new and quite lengthy journey.

*

As one considers Simon Benson's character and what made him so successful and important, one has to conclude that perhaps the most salient aspect of his personality can really only be described as *prescience* – the ability to see into the future. This is not to say that Benson was somehow psychic, but he had an exceptional skill at knowing what might come next, what the future might hold in store. He could see trends develop, and from this knowledge he could determine how best to prepare for what was coming and bring maximum benefit from it. We have seen this ability already in his life: first in 1879, when he decided to relocate himself and his family to Oregon, rightly believing a better future for logging lay there rather than in the Midwest. We see it again in the early 1890s, when he became one of the first to adopt and adapt the new steam technology that would revolutionize the logging and lumber industry. And again, this singular ability would manifest in 1906 with his realization that his products should go to Southern California and his development of the great log rafts that bore the Benson name. Benson knew the great market of the future for lumber lay to the south, and he set his sights on finding a way to make that market his own in practical and efficient as well as highly lucrative ways.

There is nothing magical about these decisions and this prescience. In each of these cases, Benson simply paid close attention to what he read, heard, and saw, and then decided for himself what seemed the likeliest next step. Then he made his decisions boldly, even fearlessly, willing to take enormous risks because of supreme confidence in his own insight.

Now having fully sold off his interests in the Benson Logging and Lumber Company, Benson further turned his interests and his ideas for the future toward his adopted home of Portland, a place which he had come to love and in which he took great pride. Benson was fascinated with engineering and technology, and not only when it came to the logging industry. The development of the automobile had caught his attention early on. As we will see in the next chapter, he understood sooner and better than many people the need for good roads in America: he recognized early how important quality roads were for getting his timber out of the forest to the rivers that transported them to mills, and from the mills to the cities he helped to build. Benson was still using a horse and carriage in the early 1900s, but by 1907 he had bought for his family a seven-passenger Peerless auto – the one daughter Alice decorated for the following year's Rose Festival Parade.

Perhaps it was the Lewis and Clark Exposition of 1905 that brought about his interest in cars because it almost certainly engendered in him a deep and abiding interest in another modern phenomenon, one that would become ever more closely related to cars: tourism. Once the railroads began to cover significant portions of the nation, people started to discover the pleasures of extended travel just for the sake of visiting interesting new places. Up until the early nineteenth century, most Americans were too busy just making a living to have much concern with traveling for fun. Some of the most wealthy could afford to do so, but Europe, taking the "Grand Tour," remained their preferred destination. The trains changed that. One of the first great American tourist attractions, Niagara Falls, fairly easily accessible from the great population centers of New York City, Boston, and Philadelphia, was by the 1860s so crowded with souvenir hawkers and annoying guides, tourists began to complain. After the Civil War, rail travel became even easier, cheaper, more widespread, and thus more open to other people besides the elite few. Among the first beneficiaries of this were the great expositions discussed previously. Hundreds of thousands of people from many walks of life flocked to St. Louis, Chicago, and even Portland, and hotels and other accommodations grew to serve them. Also, as we have seen, Benson himself and his family became avid travelers: they all enjoyed various destinations in California – his daughter Alice saying he especially loved the sunny Southland – and even Hawaii, still at that time a trip only for the very wealthy.

Because of this increase in travel, this period of the late nineteenth and early twentieth centuries saw the construction of many great, iconic hotels. The Plaza in New York City, the Grand Hotel on Mackinac Island, Michigan, the Hotel del Coronado in San Diego, the Jefferson Hotel in Richmond, Virginia, and the St. Francis Hotel in San Francisco, where Benson was rudely awakened by the great earthquake of 1906 – these and many others were built during this period and still proudly stand today; still others have faded into history. Portland itself had some fine lodging options, such as the Portland Hotel, a beautiful Queen-Anne chateau in the heart of downtown that was demolished to make way for a parking lot in the 1950s, and the Multnomah and Heathman Hotels, both of which still stand, the Multnomah now as part of the Embassy Suites chain, the Heathman still proudly keeping its own name.

While the lodging market might have seemed well supplied, Benson had other ideas. He looked at the success of the Lewis and Clark Exposition – unusually for such fairs it actually made a profit – as well as its attendance figures: more than one million five hundred thousand people paid to walk through the gates in less than five months, nearly a third coming from beyond the Pacific Northwest – a respectable number for a city whose population at the time stood at about one hundred twenty thousand. Eight hundred thousand visitors bought hotel rooms, paying anything from fifty cents up to five dollars per night. Many enjoyed their visit so much they decided to stay: between 1900 and 1910 Portland more than doubled in size, thanks in no small part to the fair's visitors and attendant publicity.

SIMON BENSON

Benson considered all of this, and he saw great potential for tourism in Oregon, especially as cars would continue to become more affordable for greater numbers of people, and more and more of the country would be connected by networks of good highways. He decided business would continue to grow and thrive in Oregon, especially in Portland, its major city, and that tourism would as well. People would come to visit this fine city and admire the natural beauty surrounding it. What Portland needed, then, was a truly magnificent hotel which would be a shining beacon for the city, a place to rival the best hotels in New York, Chicago, and San Francisco. Portland already had some good hotels; now it needed a great one. In 1912, Benson decided he would build it.

His model would be Chicago's Blackstone Hotel. Opened in 1910, the Blackstone quickly earned a reputation as setting the new standard for elegance and became popular among political figures, businessmen – that era was very much a man's world – and well-to-do travelers. For decades every single President of the United States stayed there, and during the

Early postcard of the Benson Hotel. (Benson family collection)

SIMON BENSON

1920 Republican National Convention it was the site of the famous "smoke-filled room" in which political wheelers and dealers of the Republican Party arranged among themselves the choice of congenial, corrupt Warren G. Harding as their party's presidential candidate and eventually the country's next President.

Benson admired the Blackstone's graceful architecture and beautiful décor. Once again, he called upon the talents of architect A.E. Doyle, this time to design a beautiful, Beaux Arts-style structure very similar to the Blackstone, its design featuring elements of Renaissance and Greco-Roman styles. He also asked Doyle to copy the Blackstone's mansard roof. This reflected the Second Empire school of design made popular in the mid-nineteenth century by French Emperor Napoleon III when he modernized and rebuilt much of Paris's architecture. The hotel's exterior consists of red bricks and cream-colored terra cotta. The green terra cotta and copper mansard roof rests as an ornate "cap" on the building where the hotel's penthouse suites look out over the city. While Benson's hotel resembled the Blackstone, he asked for a scaled-down version that would fit comfortably into Portland's much smaller downtown area. His new hotel would stand only twelve stories tall, rather than the Blackstone's twenty-two.

SIMON BENSON

Benson spared no expense on his hotel: it would have nothing but the finest, most beautiful, most costly decorations and amenities. Most of the woodwork throughout the hotel was mahogany with gold trim, but for the lobby he imported Circassian walnut from imperial Russia; this type of wood is now extinct. Some say the only time he had second thoughts about the extravagant construction was when he saw the bill for the Russian wood paneling, but he went ahead regardless. The floors are of Italian marble, the chandeliers of Austrian crystal. "The ceiling was punctuated with ornate plaster designs of acanthus, rosettes, egg-and-dart, and other classical motifs," one admiring historian notes. Each room had modern conveniences such as electric lights, a telephone, and a private bath, and every guest's breakfast began with a cup of hot clam juice (or "nectar"), a singularly Northwestern touch. It tastes a little better than it sounds. The larger suites contained grand pianos. Another luxurious hotel, the Multnomah, which opened around the same time,

Postcard showing the lobby as it originally looked. (Benson family collection)

had five hundred rooms; Benson's hotel had only two hundred rooms but cost the same to build.

Benson lavishly financed the hotel's construction, but he did not claim to know how to run it; his plan was to lease it to an established hotelier. When it opened in March 1913 it was under the management of the Oregon Hotel Company; the organization that already managed the neighboring Oregon Hotel. Soon the older property came to be known as the Old Oregon Hotel and Benson's edifice was called the New Oregon Hotel. However, these managers could not find a sound way to manage the new hotel, and it started to lose money. After sixteen straight months of losses, Benson took back his property and began to manage it himself. Benson said,

> Just as I studied the mistakes made in operating donkey engines and constructing sea-going rafts, I studied this hotel to learn where I could cut out waste and lost motion and improve the service and increase trade. It paid me a profit of over a hundred thousand dollars a year for the next three years. I had demonstrated to myself I could make it pay so I sold it for an even million dollars.

Evidently, Benson did not find it difficult to make the leap from building and overseeing a large logging and milling operation to building and managing a large hotel. At that time, a new philosophy called "scientific management" was sweeping through corporate America; it is sometimes referred to as "Taylorism" after one of its early proponents, Frederick Winslow Taylor. In essence, the idea was for business owners and managers to apply scientific principles of analysis and mechanization in order to maximize productivity – to find ways to ensure the most productivity from workers in the least amount of time. Taylor studied such activities as shoveling and bricklaying, looking for the optimal ways to perform each task. He coined the term "a fair day's pay for a fair day's work." While this philosophy could be hard on workers when taken to extremes – Charlie Chaplin's film *Modern Times* offers an interesting parody of ways management could abuse workers when following this philosophy – it is difficult to argue with the basic idea of reducing waste and increasing efficiency and productivity. Taylor himself called for management and workers to act as partners, and he emphasized that his ideas called for working better, not necessarily working harder.

Benson would likely have been well aware of the scientific management movement: his comments here, especially his words about cutting "lost motion," appear to come straight out of it. One could even consider Benson a pioneer of these management techniques as his adoption of new technology in the early 1890s consciously sought to increase productivity and profits. Yet his actions decades earlier as well as now with the hotel indicate another personality characteristic that many of his contemporary business owners did not share: a willingness to spend large amounts of money in order to make even more. Benson risked a great deal of money on steam donkeys, on Shay locomotives and miles of rails, on building the rafts; likewise, he now invested heavily in his hotel. Many of his contemporaries preferred to maximize profits by minimizing cost, and their workers and customers sometimes suffered because of inadequate facilities and equipment. One of Benson's first acts when he took back the business from the Oregon Hotel Company was to install an expensive new heating system. But Benson was shrewd, and he made sure his biggest gambles paid off handsomely.

Henry Thiele. (Photo courtesy of the Oregon Historical Society)

One of Benson's best acts as proprietor of the hotel was to bring in Henry Thiele as head chef in the restaurant. Thiele, born in Germany and previously employed in France and Switzerland, became Portland's "first famous chef," according to James Beard, the well-known gourmet, chef, and food writer. Beard was born in Portland and had a lasting friendship with his contemporary and schoolmate Chester Benson, Simon's youngest son. In his autobiography *Delights and Prejudices*, he notes that while Chester and his brother Gilbert lived with their mother Pamelia, now divorced from Simon, both had charge accounts at the hotel and Beard was frequently treated to lunch or dinner there. He says of Thiele that he "had a fawning manner and great ambition, but he was a great, creative chef." One wonders whether Thiele was one of the early influences that led Beard to his own outstanding career with food.

When Benson took over, he named the property after himself. Although he only operated it for a few years before selling it off, the name stuck, and it has become a Portland landmark; it was added to the National Register of Historic Places in 1986. Through a variety of corporate owners and more than one hundred years, it remains the Benson Hotel (or more formally, the Hotel Benson). Like the Blackstone, the Benson boasts of hosting many celebrities, entertainers, politicians, and virtually every United States President since William Howard Taft.

Postcard of the London Grille, the Benson Hotel restaurant. (Benson family collection)

Even as Benson settled into his new role of hotel owner and manager, events started to take his attention in a new direction – one in which his interests in technology and future tourism, as well as his love for Oregon, could flourish even further.

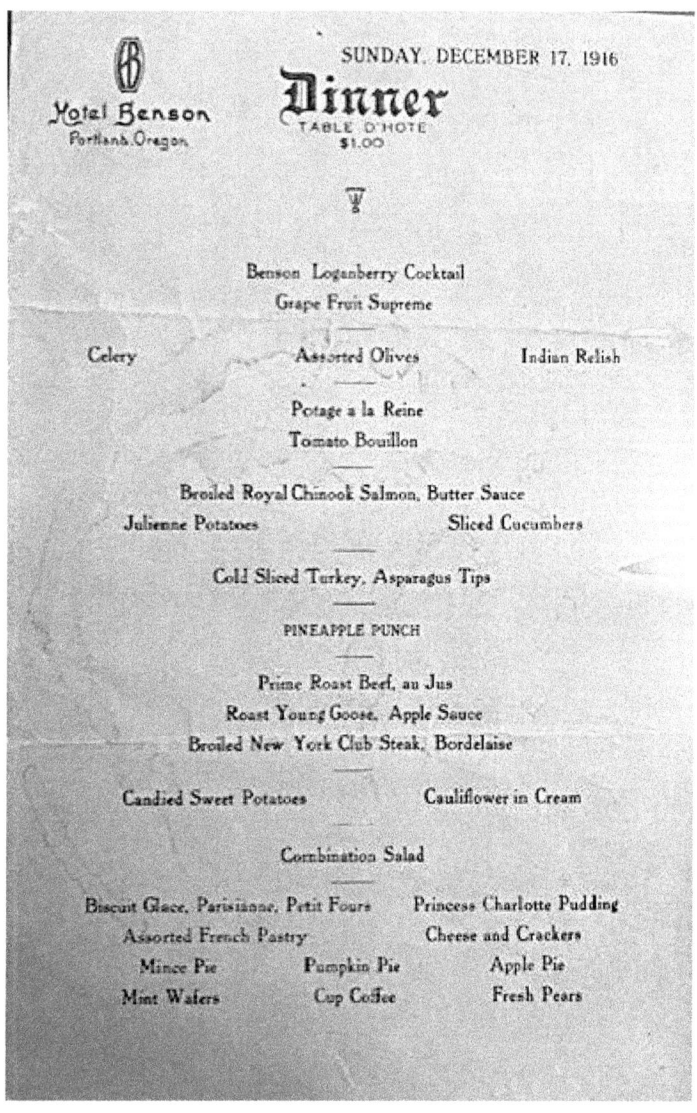

Hotel Benson holiday dinner menu, 1916. (Benson family collection)

Chapter 6: The Columbia River Scenic Highway

Simon Benson bought his first automobile in the early 1900s, but his understanding of the importance of good roads certainly predated that by many years. His business required moving large, heavy loads over great distances, and when he started, as we have seen, his industry was still in the era of using oxen and rivers for much of the hauling. It took great effort to get his fallen trees out of the forest to the lumber mills, usually over "corduroy" roads created from still more fallen trees. Much of the work was labor-intensive, dirty, and slow. Part of the movement could be effected by water, and in time Benson of course became an early adopter of railroads, But roads were still needed to get the lumber from the work site to the railheads and sometimes from the train to the river; later in the process, the milled lumber needed to be transported to the cities. Roads played a vital role in the lumber industry, and Benson was well aware of it.

In fact, he was far from the only one who understood the importance of roads and wanted to see

America's roads improved. A "Good Roads Movement" had begun in America as early as the late 1870s. At that time, while cities maintained their own streets, very few roads connected cities or towns to each other. Except for a few rare highways connecting major population centers like New York and Boston, the vast majority of American cities and towns were connected, if they were at all, by dirt tracks or occasional short gravel roads. Often, they were little more than mud in the winter and dust in the summer. In most places, for example, the famous Oregon Trail was not a trail at all, but a general route that a family or wagon train might take while others on the same route might have been heading in the same direction but miles to the left or right. Benson got a firsthand look at the poor quality of roads in Oregon during a 1910 auto trip up the Mt. Hood Highway. His daughter Alice remembered it as a nightmare: "nothing but mud and steep hills." Local farmers had to be enlisted to use their horses to pull cars out of the muck.

Car stuck in mud. (Library of Congress photo)

The first transcontinental railroad was completed in 1869, tying the East Coast and the West Coast together for the first time; by 1880, the nation's entire rail network already comprised more than ninety-three thousand miles of tracks, and in the following decade it would grow by another seventy thousand miles. Much of this growth took place in the West as population rapidly increased there. Although some people, like Benson's second wife Pamelia, still journeyed by wagon trains, railroads began to replace covered wagons for people desiring to travel across the country. When Benson brought his family west in 1879, he would most likely have taken trains from Wisconsin to San Francisco, then a steamship to Portland. This was the typical method of travel at that time. They missed being able to take trains for the entire trip by only a few years: the Northern Pacific completed its own transcontinental line linking Portland to the rest of the nation in 1883. Many considered railroads even more important for shipping goods: "The railroad system," says one historian, "answered the needs for many years of other means of transportation, except for the short distances that existed between the farms or the factories and the railroad station."

Even as the rail network proliferated, people were thinking about improving the nation's transportation systems. Business operators like Simon Benson loved the railroads and made full and efficient use of them, but they knew they still needed to get their goods to and from the trains, and into people's homes, in a country where a huge percentage of the population still lived outside cities and towns. Good roads were clearly needed. In just a couple of decades the internal-combustion engine would create an enormous demand for improved roads with the development of the automobile, but already another invention was starting to fuel the desire for easier access for city people to get to the countryside: the bicycle.

The first bicycle appeared early in the nineteenth century and consisted only of two wheels attached by a bar;

it was called a "Dandy Horse." A person would straddle it and walk or run until it was moving fast enough to "ride." Early pedal-powered bicycles were developed in Europe in the 1860s, with the pedals on the front wheel like a modern tricycle. These came to be called "boneshakers," which says something about the smoothness of their ride. The boneshaker was invented in France, as was the "penny farthing" bicycle with its very tall front wheel and much smaller real wheel; it was developed in 1869. In 1885 an Englishman named John Kemp Starley patented his "safety bicycle," known as Rover. This became the precursor to the modern bike, with its steerable front wheel and chain connecting pedals to the rear wheel. Stanley's invention launched the "Golden Age of Bicycles," during which

The "American Velocipede," illustration from Harper's Weekly, *1868. (Wikipedia image)*

riding became incredibly popular throughout Europe and America.

This new popularity of bicycling led to calls for more and better roads for people to ride on. They could use paved or cobbled streets in the cities, but they wanted more freedom of movement, the ability to explore the countryside beyond the edge of town. But the roads they needed did not exist. In Europe, national and local governments supported building convenient and scenic highways, but the United States government responded more slowly. The Good Roads Movement officially began in 1880 with the founding of the League of American Wheelmen; a group of riding clubs, bicycle manufacturers, and individual enthusiasts met in Newport, Rhode Island, to encourage the new hobby of riding and lobby for more government support. A particularly popular and successful publication from the League was *The Gospel of Good Roads: A Letter to the American Farmer*, which appeared in 1891. It exhorted the country's agricultural community to demand new roads in order to help bring products to market as well as help take children to school and families to church. In 1892 the organization began publishing *Good Roads Magazine*, which gained more than a million subscribers within just a few years. Also, in that year, a thousand people gathered in Chicago to form the National League of Good Roads. Soon the federal government began investigating new techniques of road building. At first, even the railroads supported the movement as they saw potential for drawing in more customers. Later, as cars gained popularity and started to compete, the railroad companies would regret providing this early encouragement.

The first issue of Good Roads *magazine, 1892. (Wikipedia photo)*

By the early twentieth century as the car started to grow in popularity, "automobilists" began to join the Good Roads Movement, and once Henry Ford introduced his Model T in 1908 there was no stopping them. Both the federal government and a number of state governments took notice. As traffic increased and the winter roads became muddier, taxpayers lost their reluctance to pay for new roads, and highway construction began. In 1909, the first mile of concrete highway appeared in Michigan. In 1912, construction began on the Lincoln Highway, a rock-based road that would eventually stretch from Times Square in New York City to Lincoln Park in San Francisco, becoming America's first transcontinental highway. Carl Fisher, an entrepreneur and car lover who had previously built the Indianapolis Motor Speedway, home of the Indy 500. led the push to build the Lincoln Highway and is seen today as one of the pioneers of America's road network.

Simon Benson was certainly fully conscious of these developments and supported them, and he was not the only Oregonian growing in awareness of them. As we have seen, Benson would have been in favor of building good new roads as the owner of logging and lumber operations, but he would have had other reasons as well. Thanks to his interest in new technology, he would surely have been aware from early on of the increasing popularity of the automobile. Another idea that must certainly have influenced his thinking was seeing the great success of the Lewis and Clark Centennial Exposition: more than one and a half million paying customers overall, nearly a third of them coming from beyond Oregon and Washington.

SIMON BENSON

Historians estimate the exposition brought some eight hundred thousand people to Portland hotels, each person spending approximately ten dollars during a typical three-day stay, thus bringing an extra eight million dollars to the city in a single year – beyond what they would have spent at the fairgrounds. The equivalent in today's dollars would be more than a quarter of a billion. Benson would have noticed that trains were creating a new burgeoning interest in tourism, and he would have sensed that once good roads were built, the automobile would increase that interest even more. Once he sold his ownership in his lumber operations and began to explore his new interests, building roads became perhaps his favorite, the one to which he devoted the most time and attention.

*

While Benson would go on to become a champion of roads throughout Oregon, particularly the road that become Oregon's portion of US Highway 30, which would eventually become a transcontinental route, his special area of interest from the beginning would be creating a road through the Columbia River Gorge. The Columbia, the "great river of the west," flows more than twelve hundred miles from its headwaters in Canada, through eastern and central Washington, and eventually forms the border between Washington and Oregon before it finally empties into the Pacific Ocean. It drains an area of two hundred fifty-nine thousand square miles, about the size of France, from seven states and British Columbia, Canada. Every second, it discharges an average of almost one hundred ninety-five thousand gallons of water, second in America only to the Mississippi. Lewis and Clark, as well as other early European and American explorers, hoped to find a connection between the Missouri and Columbia rivers as they sought a Northwest Passage, a water route that would cross the American continent. They were disappointed in that, but still impressed by the great size of the river.

The Columbia Gorge is the name of the seventy-five-mile stretch of the river from The Dalles on the eastern side of the Cascade Mountains westward to Troutdale, at the eastern edge of Portland. Massive floods twelve to fifteen thousand years ago created the only passage close to sea level through the large interior mountain ranges that extend down the continent from Canada to Mexico. As the river flows through the Cascade Range, it narrows into a passage only about three miles wide with thousand-foot-tall hills and cliffs on either side. It is a place of immense and intense natural beauty: it is "almost congested with scenic views – mountain peaks, waterfalls, plateaus, orchards, and wheatfields," says Alice Benson Allen.

From the start people admired the gorge for its scenery; however, the river was deadly. While ships could navigate the Columbia above and below the gorge, two major rapids prevented navigation within the gorge. Celilo Falls near The Dalles was a sacred Native American fishing spot but an absolute barricade for boats; Cascade Rapids, some forty-five miles upriver from Portland and a similar distance downstream from The Dalles, also proved virtually impassable for watercraft. These rapids and falls were both spectacular and clearly perilous. During the Lewis and Clark Expedition, William Clark rode the falls at The Dalles in a canoe. Native Americans lined the banks to watch, convinced that he would be killed. As white settlers arrived on the Oregon Trail, after walking for months over thousands of miles, they found the last one hundred miles the most difficult, dangerous, and terrifying. Many took the treacherous overland route once they learned the alternative: those who tried to follow the river toward Portland could either remove the wheels from their wagons and brave the river on rafts, which was every bit as dangerous as it sounds, or they had to empty their wagons and portage all their goods around both sets of rapids. This led to delays, increased expenses, and the possibility of losing property to theft.

Eventually, the Columbia was tamed when canals were built around the rapids. First the Cascade Canal opened in 1896. Steamboats were able to make the journey from Portland to Hood River in about twelve hours, using locks to get past the Cascade Rapids; the town of Cascade Locks now stands on this site. However, they could not get past the bigger, more powerful rapids at The Dalles until the twentieth century, when the Dalles-Celilo Canal opened in 1915. Finally, a ship was able to make the trip all the way from Lewiston, Idaho, to Portland. In the years since, massive dams have tamed the Columbia and the falls and rapids are deep underwater; today's visitors see only a huge, placid river and have no idea what difficulties their ancestors faced.

Railroads also appeared in the Columbia Gorge. In 1851, an entrepreneur named Harden Chenoweth put a cart on wheels on the north side of the river at the Cascade Rapids and created a "portage tramway." A donkey pulled the cart, carrying freight at seventy-five cents per hundred pounds. Real portage railroads around the great rapids were completed by 1863. The "Oregon Pony," the first steam-powered engine in the Pacific Northwest, replaced the donkey-pulled train at the portage around Cascade Rapids in 1862. In 1882, the Oregon Rail and Navigation Company successfully completed a line through the gorge from eastern Oregon all the way to Portland, just above the high-water line of the river; it later became part of the Union Pacific's national network. The Spokane, Portland, and Seattle Railroad completed a parallel line along the Washington side of the Columbia in 1908. Once the railroads made the Columbia Gorge more easily accessible, early tourists started to come from Portland to visit the gorge by train as well as, in some areas, by boat.

SIMON BENSON

Train in the Columbia River Gorge, c. 1885. (Photo courtesy of the Oregon Historical Society)

While travel and shipping through the Columbia Gorge improved slowly, once cars became important many state leaders, planners, and visionaries, including Simon Benson, began to see a need for a highway through the gorge. However, the nature of the terrain made actual construction a formidable challenge. The Native Americans who had lived in the area for thousands of years had created a few trails, but nothing the white planners of the nineteenth century would consider suitable as the basis for a road. Likewise, a few early settlers had created tracks that were little better for the immigrants' wagons. The first serious attempt to build a road running the full length of the gorge started in 1872, when the Oregon State Legislature appropriated fifty thousand dollars for a wagon road running from The Dalles to the mouth of the Sandy River near Troutdale at the opening of the gorge; another appropriation of fifty thousand dollars more followed in 1876. The resulting road was considered inadequate: it was "crooked, rugged, and steep." Construction of the Oregon Rail and Navigation Company railroad in the early 1880s wiped out much of this early road; only "a few traces" could be found by the early 1900s.

*

One of the major difficult points along the route was Shellrock Mountain, an imposing point more than two thousand feet high that stands on the bank of the river west of the city of Hood River. Early pioneers on the Oregon Trail considered it impassable and stopped on its eastern flank to cut trees and build rafts to go around it. Due to the mountain's steepness and its loose rocky slopes, the first road from the 1870s proved impossible to maintain. Every supporter of a new, improved gorge highway knew Shellrock Mountain would be a serious impediment to fulfilling their dreams.

Shellrock Mountain, with steamship landing at its base. (Photo courtesy of the Oregon Historical Society)

In fact, the next attempt to build a road around the mountain would also prove a failure, but it is significant because it marked Simon Benson's first appearance on the road-building scene. In 1912, Benson gave Governor Oswald West ten thousand dollars to finance an experimental project that would have laborers from the Oregon State Prison attempt to build a new road around Shellrock Mountain. There being no state Highway Commission in Oregon at the time, West directed the scheme be undertaken and largely paid for by Hood River County, using state prisoners. Benson's money was only enough to get things started.

The effort failed; the prisoners did not complete their road around Shellrock Mountain, perhaps due to lack of expertise and insufficient engineering skills. As soon as the road was completed it began to fall apart. However, from the project's ashes came great success. First, the effort created fresh enthusiasm in Oregon for a new, better road to be built along the entire length of the gorge. The excitement especially started growing in Multnomah County, the home of Portland and the financial center of the state. Businessmen began expressing support for a good highway to connect the eastern and western halves of the state and to show off one of its most scenic areas.

The second profound effect of the Shellrock Mountain failure was that it sparked particular interest in the heart and soul of Simon Benson: he had discovered a new passion. He soon became one of the leading proponents of good roads not only in the Columbia Gorge but throughout Oregon. He was an official member of the Good Roads Movement organization, and he met with prominent fellow good-roads advocates in Portland and across the state and found plenty of support. Among those Portlanders who were especially enthusiastic were Henry Pittock and Sam Jackson, publishers of the *Oregonian* and *Journal* respectively, Portland's leading newspapers; fellow lumber baron John Yeon; and department-store magnate Julius Meier, who as president of the Columbia Highway Association encouraged building a highway not only through the gorge but all the way from Astoria on the coast to Pendleton in eastern Oregon, a distance of some three hundred forty miles.

*

The Columbia Gorge Highway's biggest proponent, however, was not a Portlander or even an Oregonian. Sam Hill, formerly a lawyer for the Great Northern Railroad, had married the boss's daughter and done very well for himself. He traveled extensively in Europe, making more than thirty trips there, as well as several journeys to Asia; he spoke fluent German, French, and Italian; and he counted among his friends Queen Marie of Rumania (as the country's name was then spelled), King Leopold of Belgium, and Alma Spreckels who was one of the great benefactors of San Francisco's art and culture. Hill also had several mistresses and a number of illegitimate children.

Sam Hill, 1915. (Wikimedia photo)

Eventually he relocated from Minneapolis to Seattle, where he found a lasting love for the Pacific Northwest. In 1899 he became the first president of the Washington State Good Roads Association. After some years serving as director or president of various companies, including Seattle Gas and Electric and subsidiaries of the Great Northern, Hill began to focus less on business and more on personal interests. He retired or resigned from most of the companies and turned more toward real estate and stock speculation, at which he proved highly adept. And he continued to advocate for good roads; this included testimony before the U.S. Senate. By the 1900s he was widely known as the "the Father of Good Roads." In 1904 he sold off the gas and electric business and devoted himself to advocating for the Washington State Legislature to build good roads.

Hill had come to love the rolling hills of central Washington, and in 1907 he bought seven thousand acres of land on the Columbia River, a few miles east of the end of the gorge. He called his estate Maryhill, named for his daughter. (His wife was also named Mary, but she and Hill were estranged; while they had not divorced, their marriage had deteriorated over the years, and they had largely lived apart.) He built an enormous mansion on a hill above the river and he also took over a nearby small town that he tried to organize on strict conservative and puritanical principles. He was concerned about the allure of big cities tempting young people to leave farm life:

> I believe in man on the land. We cannot afford to have our producers leave the land and become parasites. We want our girls to stay on the farm and become mothers of a virile race of men and not just go to the city and become manicurists, stenographers, and variety actresses. We want our boys to stay on the farm and not succumb to the lure of the Great White Way or become chauffeurs and clerks. We cannot keep the ambitious boy or girl on the farm unless we make life attractive and comfortable.

Good roads played a central role in Hill's desire to keep people on the land. "[O]nly through good roads can people be put upon the land and kept there," he said. Unless people stayed on the land, "government cannot last. Civilization cannot last if Government does not."

Samuel Lancaster. (Wikipedia photo)

"Good roads are more than my hobby, they are my religion," Hill said.

Hill soon started lobbying the Washington State Legislature to build a road through the Columbia Gorge on the northern side of the river, both to offer better access to Maryhill and to create what would clearly become a significant scenic route. This lobbying effort was ultimately unsuccessful, but then he met another Sam, an engineer named Samuel C. Lancaster. They formed a partnership that would make history.

Lancaster had a remarkable life story. He had studied engineering briefly at college, but financial exigencies forced him to complete his education in the real world, first with the Illinois Central Railroad. As a young man he first overcame a severe case of typhoid fever, and then a bout of polio that left him without the use of his arms or legs; it was already remarkable that Lancaster had survived these diseases at all. At least as much as Esther Benson's diagnosis of tuberculosis, either typhoid fever or polio, known then as "infantile paralysis," would have been considered a likely death sentence in the nineteenth century. Doctors told him the nerves in his extremities were dead, but this proved incorrect. Through sheer force of will, Lancaster gradually taught himself to write again and to create engineering diagrams. He gave much of the credit for overcoming his illness to his deep religious faith. After he recovered, he began a remarkably successful career as an engineer for Madison County, Mississippi, and the city of Jackson where he had spent most of his life. Still in his twenties, he oversaw the development of paved roads, sewers, parks, and other projects, always keeping meticulous records. Eventually the city of Jackson named a park for him.

His outstanding work on roads in Mississippi brought Lancaster to the attention of James Wilson, the U.S. Secretary of Agriculture, who brought him to Washington, D.C., and made him the consulting engineer for the Bureau of Good Roads. He was perfect for the job.

Lancaster, as a biographer put it, combined "extreme engineering skill and a reverence for beauty and the God who created it in the same man." Wilson sent him across the country to "preach the gospel of good roads." Eventually, on one of these tours, Samuel Lancaster met Sam Hill. Hill persuaded Lancaster to move from the nation's capital to Washington state, first working on a major development of parks and streets in preparation for the Alaska-Yukon-Pacific Exposition, another world's fair, that Seattle would host in 1909. Hill also successfully lobbied the University of Washington to name Lancaster its Chair of Highway Engineering. But in spite of getting him these positions, Hill, who had been a member of the Washington State Highway Board for some time, had other plans for Lancaster.

In 1908, the two men traveled to Europe, along with Reginald H. Thomson and Henry R. Bowlby, other Washington engineers. The occasion for the trip was to attend the First International Road Congress in Paris. This conference established the international organization now called the World Road Association, but for the visitors from the Pacific Northwest, the highlight of their trip came after the conference, when they began a lengthy trip by car through much of Europe. There they saw how government-supported roads could offer both convenience for farm and business shipments and access to beautiful scenery to everyone. Hill and Lancaster returned to the United States more convinced than ever of the need for good American roads.

Hill made little headway in his efforts to convince the Washington State Legislature to build a road on the Washington side of the Columbia River Gorge. Like Simon Benson and Oregon Governor Oswald West, he saw great potential in the use of convict labor. On one occasion he said to *The New York Times*, "P.D. Armour [the meat-packing titan] once told me that no great manufacturing corporation could prosper unless it utilized its by-products. I believe the same to be true of society. One of the society's by-products is the convict. Our utilization of him in the construction of our roads is strictly along efficiency lines." Like Benson, Hill also must have been well aware of the "scientific management" philosophy that was then sweeping the country.

Unfortunately for Hill, if not for the convicts, some Washington legislators did not agree with him. A number of others withdrew their support for the gorge road upon learning that even with convict labor, it would cost an estimated thirty thousand dollars per mile. The Washington road plan died before it could even begin. Therefore, he decided to turn his attention to Oregon. He and Lancaster created a headquarters at the Arlington Club in Portland, soon joined by Simon Benson, and began to tour the state whipping up enthusiasm for their proposed projects, which already included a major north-south highway running all the way from Canada to Mexico as well as the east-west highway through the gorge.

Early in 1913, Hill brought Governor West and the entire Oregon State Legislature, along with some other guests, to Maryhill by train and showed them an amazing sight. Since 1911, he had spent one hundred thousand dollars for Lancaster to use the large property as a testing site for building roads using various paving techniques and materials. These ten miles of experimental roads still exist, and one in particular, known as the Maryhill Loops Road, served as a proving ground for the techniques that would be used in building the Columbia Gorge Highway. The Maryhill Loops Road, which its supporters claim was the first asphalt-paved road in the Pacific Northwest, rises eight hundred fifty feet over three point six miles and includes twenty-five curves including several hairpins. Most important, the road maintained a grade of no more than five percent, a gentle and manageable slope. This was crucial for the comfort and safety of passengers in cars of the era, and Lancaster had proved it could be done. By comparison, the road of the 1870s had included grades of twelve percent and some other early bits of road in the gorge were built at an extremely steep twenty-two percent. Governor West and the legislators were impressed, and the highway received their blessing. The project had the official green light. The legislature passed a law allowing counties to issue bonds in order to raise money for road building. At this time, Oregon had no state highway commission, but Oswald West soon remedied that. He persuaded the Oregon State Legislature to create a commission and named Simon Benson its chairman; the commission named Hill's colleague Henry R. Bowlby the state highway engineer. However, funding for the project would have to come from the counties involved, as had been the case when West and Benson had tried to build a road over Shellrock Mountain the year before; it would take time for the state to start paying for road construction.

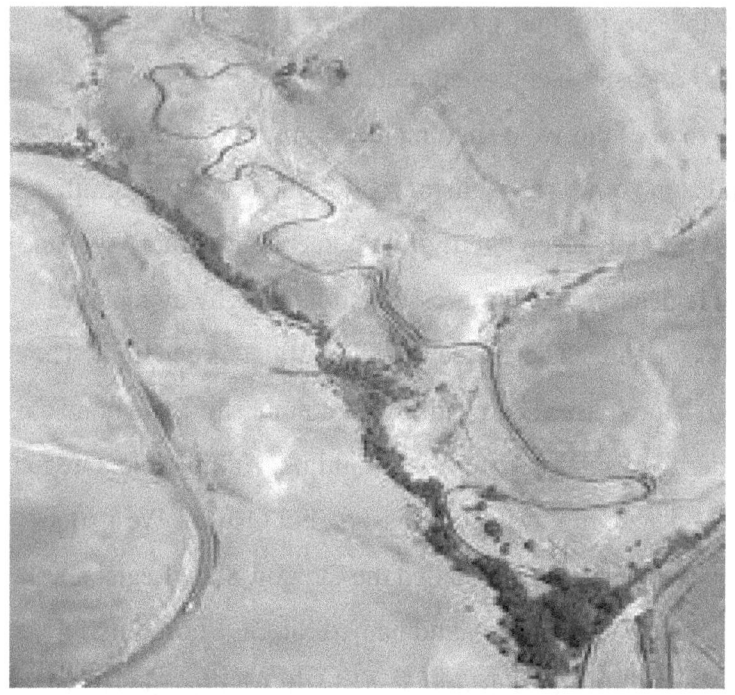

The Maryhill Loops Road. (Wikipedia photo)

*

Thanks to the Maryhill Loops Road, everyone could see that the highway could be built through the gorge. Simon Benson and the other Portland business leaders stepped up and lent their enthusiastic support to the project. "As far as the highway was concerned, if Sam Hill was the 'spark plug,' Benson provided the gas," one observer remarks. On 26 July 1913, the Multnomah County

Commissioners voted to establish an Advisory Board on Roads and Highways. The board's membership included Hill as well as Amos Benson, who had gained training in civil engineering. On 27 August of that year, at a special meeting at the Chanticleer Inn, a venue not far outside Portland on the mountains above the gorge, the Multnomah County Commissioners voted to support construction of the highway, including putting forth seventy-five thousand dollars for initial surveying. The following day they named Lancaster consulting engineer for the project. While Bowlby was a good engineer and an interesting character – he rose to the rank of "Major" during World War I despite having been expelled from West Point – Lancaster would truly be the person responsible for the highway's design. It would become a byword for scenic beauty and a harmonious synthesis that allowed the road to fit beautifully with the surrounding natural scenery.

Amos Benson. (Photo courtesy of the Oregon Historical Society)

Lancaster insisted that "the best modern practice should be followed in building a road suited to the times, the traffic, and the place." He said the road must be twenty-four feet wide and have grades of no more than five percent with extra-wide, gentle curves with a radius of at least one hundred feet. With road building still in its infancy in the United States, this was truly extravagant construction. One or two dissenters considered the price too high, but the majority overruled them. Lancaster even went out of his way to protect the Columbia Gorge's natural beauty to emphasize the highway's scenic nature. "I pledged that none of this wild beauty should be marred where it could be prevented," he said. "The highway would be built so that not one tree was felled, not one fern crushed, unnecessarily." Lancaster's design called for gracefully arched bridges and arched walls built by Italian stonemasons. On their trip to Europe, Hill and Lancaster had been deeply impressed by the tunnels of Switzerland's Axenstrasse highway and the ancient retaining walls on Italian roads; some dated to the time of Charlemagne. Lancaster sought to recreate this beauty as authentically as possible. Hill had imported the stonemasons for a project in Massachusetts. Eventually he abandoned that project as he focused more and more on construction in the west, but he had brought the stonemasons to Maryhill to work on the roads there, and now he invited the masons to Oregon promising good pay, room, and board.

The Axenstrasse in Switzerland. (Wikipedia photo)

Sam Hill provided the motivating force, and Samuel Lancaster the design. Simon Benson's role in the highway's creation was not so easy to categorize but it was no less important. As Chairman of the Highway Commission, he toured the state building up enthusiasm for all kinds of road building, including the stretches of the Columbia Highway from the coast to Portland and the gorge, and from Hood River onward to eastern Oregon. Benson also worked as the booster in chief in the Portland business community, building and maintaining enthusiasm and donations. As we have seen, several of the most prominent had already come forward. John B. Yeon was appointed roadmaster for the highway construction, an honorary position for which he took a salary of one dollar a year. Amos Benson helped build enthusiasm, including leading a delegation of dignitaries from farther down the Columbia to see the work in progress; much of his contribution to the highway focused on the stretch from Portland to Astoria on the coast, because of his closeness to the downriver communities like Clatskanie where what had once been the Benson Logging and Lumber operation was still going strong. He also acted as assistant roadmaster under Yeon. While the lower road cannot be compared to the magnificent highway through the gorge, its construction offered challenges of its own.

The Columbia River Highway during construction. (Photo courtesy of the Oregon Historical Society)

Others were happy to contribute in ways great and small. In the midst of the construction, on 25 April 1914, designated "Good Roads Day," five hundred Portland businessmen each paid seventy-five cents to ride a train up the gorge and work on the road for five hours; this saved the county a thousand dollars. Loans and outright gifts kept the project going until tax levies could pick up the burden. Finally, on 14 April 1915, Multnomah County voters approved a bond issue of one point two five million dollars for paving of the highway using an expensive new kind of tarmac called Warrenite; this alone cost about fifteen thousand dollars per mile. Lancaster called Warrenite "ideal for highways" and "the most economic and satisfactory material that can be used." Benson promised the people of Hood River County that if they would approve a seventy-five-thousand-dollar bond measure, he would personally pay for any cost overruns. In fact, after the measure passed handily, he went ahead and bought the entire bond issue himself. It was a great era for philanthropy.

A worker named Sam Hulit carries a wagonload of Warrenite to the construction site. (Photo from Troutdale Historical Museum)

Another episode that nicely illustrates Benson's role in the project came when a particular landowner was unable to reach agreement with Multnomah County to sell his property. The two parties reached an impasse and the landowner posted "No Trespassing" signs, virtually halting construction. Whatever the actual amount in question might have been, at one public meeting at the Chanticleer Inn the county representatives said they could not increase their offer to buy the man's land any further and the property owner would not accept a penny less than his final demand. At this, on the spur of the moment Benson pulled out a hundred-dollar bill from his wallet and added it to the county's offer. This satisfied the landowner, the signs were removed, and construction resumed.

The Rowena loops on the highway. Experiments on the Maryhill Loops Road led to the highway's excellent construction. (Wikipedia photo)

Benson and his fellow business owners certainly had noble motives and a great desire to do good for their city and state, but one has to admit that altruism was likely not their sole motivation. Benson had opened the hotel that bore his name in Portland in 1912, not least because he believed that the increasing numbers of automobile owners, combined with the advent of good roads, would lead to a lucrative rise in the new tourism business. The gorge was already a favorite destination for Portlanders to visit, and Benson had seen many visitors come to the Pacific Northwest from across the country for the Lewis and Clark Exposition of 1905 and the even greater success of the Alaska-Yukon-Pacific Exposition of 1909 in Seattle, which some three point seven million people attended. Benson was aware of these big numbers, and he knew the biggest and best was yet to come. In 1915, San Francisco would host the Panama-Pacific International Exposition celebrating the opening of the Panama Canal and showcasing San Francisco's phoenix-like rise from the ashes of the 1906 earthquake and subsequent devastating fire. This would involve celebration on a truly epic scale; despite World War One taking place in Europe (America would not join the war until 1917), almost nineteen million visitors from all over the world would attend the San Francisco fair.

Benson foresaw that many of the visitors to San Francisco would take the opportunity to tour other parts of the American West, which by now was well connected by railroads. He also believed that touring in cars – where one could do so – would be still more popular. From the start of construction of the Columbia Gorge Highway in 1913, its builders and backers worked to complete the project by the summer of 1915. In the end, their timing would prove very nearly perfect: the road opened to traffic from Portland to Hood River on 6 July 1915, although considerable work remained to be done. The continuation of the highway, connecting Portland to Astoria on the Pacific Ocean, opened almost exactly a month later. A formal grand opening was scheduled for Labor Day Weekend, exactly two months later in early September.

*The Mitchell Point Tunnel on the highway.
(Wikimedia photo)*

SIMON BENSON

*

The heart of the Columbia Gorge, its scenic highlight, has always been Multnomah Falls. In total, it stands more than six hundred feet high; the spectacular upper falls at some five hundred forty feet, the lower falls nearly seventy. Overall, it ranks among the tallest waterfalls in the country. A Native American legend indicates that the site has been considered a place of power as well as beauty for many centuries. The story tells of a local chief who had a beautiful daughter. She was engaged to marry a warrior from a neighboring tribe, and the chief hosted a great feast for everyone in the area. During the feast, however, people began to die for reasons no one could determine. The chief called a council, during which a shaman told of a prophecy his own father had made many years before. All the people would die, he said, unless a virgin willingly sacrificed herself. Many girls of the village offered themselves, including the chief's daughter, but the chief refused to make such a sacrifice and called on everyone to face the mysterious illness bravely.

Multnomah Falls. (Photo by author)

The chief's daughter's fiancé soon became one of the sick, and that night the girl climbed the trail to the top of the high cliff to grieve for the many losses. She asked the gods for guidance. She saw the moon rise gloriously over the trees. Taking this for a sign, she threw herself off the cliff. That night the deaths stopped. The next morning, the chief asked for a sign that his daughter's death had ended the illness and that she had been accepted into the realm of the gods. At that moment, water began to flow over the cliff, and it has never stopped since.

Lewis and Clark in their journal had admired Multnomah Falls as they canoed past, and the later white settlers loved the falls too. Thanks to its location only thirty miles from central Portland, it became a favorite stop for steamboats and then excursion trains. Benson knew easy access to Multnomah Falls would have to be a key selling point for travelers on the new highway, and it became central to the planning from the start. In fact, it was the site of the initial groundbreaking despite its location miles away from the Portland end of the route.

Once construction was going strong, Benson had a wonderful brainstorm: he began to buy up the land around the falls. Some people worried that the falls would become commercialized, with hot-dog stands, games, and other gaudy attractions, as had happened at Niagara Falls previously. Benson bought up about a thousand acres around the falls that included at least one other waterfall and much lovely park land. Eventually, on Labor Day, 6 September 1915, at the official dedication of the highway, he donated one hundred sixty acres immediately surrounding Multnomah Falls and several hundred more acres nearby to the city of Portland. The original plan called for naming it Benson Park, but to this day it is just known as Multnomah Falls.

Portion of souvenir map of the new highway showing "Benson Park." 1915. (Photo by author)

SIMON BENSON

At a ceremony at the falls, at which the entire highway was formally dedicated, Benson said:

> In presenting this park to the people of the City of Portland, I had two objectives in view: first, to provide a recreation ground for the common people and their children in the city of my adoption, where they could enjoy at any time, as their own forever, one of the beauty spots of the famous Columbia River Gorge, made accessible by easy rail, river, and highway transportation.
>
> Second, as an added charm to a highway, the construction of which is the fulfillment of my fondest dreams, a highway which will soon take its place among the most noted of the world and which will put Portland and the beautiful Columbia River Gorge on the map for all time to come.

Press coverage of the dedication was ecstatic, with the Portland *Oregon Daily Journal* newspaper making much of its keeping the story up to the minute thanks to messages carried by homing pigeons. Considering the park lies about twenty miles east of the Portland city limits of today – and it was even farther at the time of the donation – the city determined it was not really appropriate as a city park and sensibly donated the entire plot of land to the U.S. Forest Service in the 1930s; that organization still administers it. Today Multnomah Falls is Oregon's most popular natural attraction with more than two million visitors from around the world each year. There is no charge for admission.

Still another ceremony, a "National Dedication," took place on 7 June 1916. For this occasion, President Woodrow Wilson in the White House in Washington, D.C., pressed a button to "close a circuit reaching across the Continent." The closing circuit caused an American flag to unfurl at Crown Point, another highlight spot in the Columbia Gorge. At this "official" dedication ceremony, attendees were served loganberry juice, the preferred beverage of Oregon's temperance movement.

SIMON BENSON

Plaque honoring Benson at Multnomah Falls.
(Photo by author)

Benson is honored by a plaque at the viewing platform at the base of the falls and a display in the visitor's center. A bridge across the pond that feeds the lower falls also bears his name. A wooden "bowstring truss" bridge was built in about 1884; surviving photographs make it appear absolutely terrifying. It was reinforced in 1891 but had decayed and fallen into Multnomah Creek at the base of the falls by 1899. One day in 1914, Benson and Samuel Lancaster were touring the falls, and Lancaster, knowing Benson's plans for the area, suggested building a beautiful new bridge. The story goes that Benson asked Lancaster how much it would cost, and Lancaster made some calculations on the back of an envelope. Benson then offered then and there to pay the estimated twenty-five-thousand-dollar cost. Sometimes this story is conflated with the one about Benson contributing a hundred dollars to buy the land from the recalcitrant property owner; sometimes one hears of him pulling out his checkbook and writing Lancaster's big check on the spot. Unfortunately, it did not happen that way, but Benson still demonstrated his largesse. Once again, he called on his friend, architect A.E. Doyle, to design the bridge. It blends harmoniously with the waterfall and references the distinctive highway design as well. Today it is known as the Benson Footbridge.

The Benson Footbridge across Multnomah Falls. (Photo by author)

The Columbia Gorge Scenic Highway as a whole was an immediate success and received rave reviews from across the country and beyond. In her book *Mighty Engineering Feats,* Harriet Elizabeth Salt placed the highway alongside other American engineering marvels such as the Panama Canal, Boulder Dam, and the Golden Gate Bridge. Writing for the *Illustrated London News,* the artist and correspondent Frederic Villiers gave the road its most lasting nickname. "It possesses the best of the great highways of the world," he said. "It is the King of Roads."

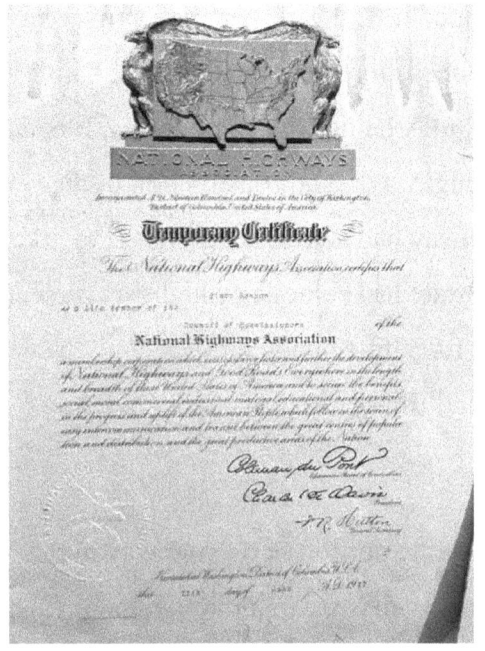

Certificate naming Simon Benson to the Council of Commissioners of the National Highways Association. (Benson family collection)

As late as 1916, only three counties in Oregon had paved roads in rural areas: Multnomah, Clatsop on the Oregon coast, and Jackson in the south. Even the Columbia River Highway was paved only as far as Multnomah Falls. At a ceremony at Rowena, several miles east of Hood River, on 27 June 1922, Benson himself spread the last shovelful of paving for the last stretch of the Columbia Gorge portion of the highway. The road at that point extended all the way to Astoria in the west to The Dalles, and it would soon progress farther. It is now part of U.S. Highway 30 which includes part of the Lincoln Highway, America's first real interstate road. It stretches more than three thousand miles from Astoria, Oregon, to Atlantic City, New Jersey. It is one of America's longest highways. The construction of the Columbia Gorge Highway had started a significant trend in Oregon: by 1920, the state had some forty highway projects going, totaling nearly forty-five hundred miles. Only New York, Pennsylvania, and Illinois were spending more on highways.

Today, much of the portion of the highway in the Columbia River Gorge has disappeared through the ravages of time and lack of maintenance since most of the traffic now follows the less scenic but much faster Interstate 84. While it once took most of a day to make the drive from Portland to Hood River through forests, over hills, and around curves, on the freeway beside the river a nonstop trip takes just little more than an hour. Some parts of the old highway have been brought back as paths for hikers and bicyclists. But one of the very best stretches, from above Crown Point to just beyond Multnomah Falls, remains intact and is well worth the detour. Today this entire route is known as the Historic Columbia River Highway.

*

Benson also contributed generously to another main attraction of the Columbia Gorge. During the highway's construction, Lancaster had proposed putting an "observatory" at Crown Point, a seven-hundred-fifty-foot exposed bluff overlooking the gorge about eight miles west of Multnomah Falls, previously known as Thor's Heights. It provides possibly the best of all views of the gorge's beauty, and Lancaster with his keen eye for nature's splendor wanted a structure "from which the view both up and down the Columbia could be viewed in silent communion with the Infinite." He also proposed that the structure could serve as a "comfort station," an "Isle of Safety to all the visitors who wish to look on that matchless scene." In other words, Lancaster was calling for something entirely new: the nation's first highway rest area. Some called it the "'Queen of Rest Stops' for the 'King of Roads.'"

There was considerable difficulty obtaining funding for this new project as there was still no money forthcoming from the state and Multnomah County had grown tired of supporting these expensive projects. Lancaster had been dismissed as the county's road builder as part of this fiscal backlash. While the price tag for the building had been set at one hundred thousand dollars, which would prove insufficient, initial fundraising efforts brought in only four thousand dollars, much of that from schoolchildren. Once again, Benson led the way in donating to the new construction, even to the extent of ensuring the highest quality materials were used. Architect Edgar M. Lazarus designed the building both to fit in with the rest of the highway and to offer an example of modern German architecture which resembled Art Nouveau. The same Italian masons who had worked on the highway, still living in Portland, laid the foundations. While much of the building is made of sandstone, Alaskan marble was used on the floors, staircases, and wainscoting. Although Lancaster was no longer an official member of the road project, he is remembered with a plaque on the façade. The building, named Vista House, had its grand opening on 5 May 1918, as usual with many dignitaries in attendance including Simon Benson. The final cost of the structure went far beyond the original hundred-thousand-dollar estimate.

SIMON BENSON

Postcard showing Vista House dedication, 1918. (Photo by author)

*

How much did Benson give to the construction of Vista House, and to the entire Columbia Gorge Scenic Highway Project? Benson, usually very precise in his memory of dollar figures and the specifics of his transactions, said, "Another investment I got a lot of pleasure and good out of was two hundred thousand dollars that I put in in building parks and roads for the pleasure and good of all the people." That seems like a good but unusually rough estimate and may even be low: a plaque honoring the most generous donors to the building and later renovation of Vista House, still gracing a wall there, places Benson almost by himself in the category of fifty to one hundred thousand dollars; the prominence of his name on the plaque suggests his donation must have been on the high end. (The only donor among Benson's contemporaries who stands higher on the plaque is Henry Pittock, publisher of the *Oregonian* newspaper. He apparently gave upwards of two hundred fifty thousand dollars.) If we combine this figure with the seventy-five thousand dollars he paid for the Hood River County bond issue and the twenty-five thousand he paid for the bridge over Multnomah Falls, we already approach his estimate. And this comes before we consider how much he must have paid for Multnomah Falls and the surrounding property, the ten thousand he offered to subsidize the failed Shellrock Mountain project of 1912, and other donations he made. He gave twenty-five thousand dollars to help fund a section of the Lower Columbia Highway near his old stomping grounds on Beaver Creek outside Clatskanie where he had seen early success as a lumberman. In fact, the old cabin he had moved into in 1888 was still standing, long abandoned; the highway passed within 100 feet of it. If anything, Benson's estimate of two hundred thousand dollars seems uncharacteristically low: he was not generally shy or vague about discussing how much money he made or spent. And we might also take into account the money he raised as the road project's strongest promoter. Benson may surely be called the highway's and the gorge's most enthusiastic cheerleader and its most generous donor. Why in this case he chose not to be more specific remains a mystery.

Chapter 7: Final Honors, Final Contributions, and "Retirement"

Nineteen-fifteen was a significant year for Simon Benson. He had secured his place in Oregon's history. He was not universally loved: one commentator described him as "intolerant and hard to get along with." One imagines he did not suffer fools or unnecessary setbacks gladly. However, he would be remembered years later by the same writer as doing "wonderful work" and being "a man of the hour when an experienced organizer was needed." As we have seen, he received considerable adulation from the state of Oregon for his contributions to the Scenic Columbia River Highway. He was one of the main featured guests of honor at various celebrations, and he was a popular speaker on the subjects of building good roads and doing good deeds. But the honors would not end with naming a park and a bridge for him. That summer of 1915 he was named "the most popular man in Oregon and the man who has accomplished the most for his state." Perhaps his greatest distinction, however, was bestowed on him that summer in California.

Simon Benson, 1915. (Photo courtesy of the San Francisco Public Library)

The Panama-Pacific International Exposition took place in San Francisco, celebrating American exceptionalism and particularly the recent completion of the Panama Canal. Although the festival had been in the planning stages since 1904, San Franciscans also saw it as an opportunity to show off their city's resurrection after the terrible earthquake and devastating fire that leveled the city in 1906. While previous world's fairs on the West Coast – another in San Francisco in 1894, the Lewis and Clark Centennial and American Pacific Exposition and Oriental Fair in Portland in 1905, Seattle's Alaska Yukon Pacific Exposition in 1909 – had done well, the 1915 fair dwarfed them in ambition, size, and attendance. It drew several times as many visitors as the others. Forty countries and colonies participated with exhibits and buildings, along with more than twenty-five American states and protectorates; even New York City had a building of its own. Some landmark structures, most famously the Palace of Fine Arts, still stand in San Francisco as remnants of the fair. Oregon's contribution was a magnificent recreation of the ancient Parthenon in Athens, built entirely of wood, with forty-two-foot pillars of Douglas fir all around. There were comparisons to the Forestry Building from Portland's Lewis and Clark exposition of a decade earlier, for which Benson provided the timber. The "Rustic Parthenon" in San Francisco received an architectural award from exposition officials.

The Oregon Building at the Panama-Pacific International Exposition, 1915. (Photo courtesy of the San Francisco Public Library)

SIMON BENSON

Seventeen August 1915 was designated the biggest day of "Oregon Week" at the fair, and at a well-attended ceremony Benson was honored by Oregon Governor James Withycombe and others as Oregon's "most distinguished and worthy citizen." A photo of the event shows Benson surrounded by politicians, aged Oregon pioneers, and other dignitaries, on a platform above several hundred onlookers. Governor Withycombe called Benson "a clean man, a man of ideals and the highest type of citizenship, the kind we are ever ready to exalt." Withycombe went on to say, in a fine example of the hyperbolic oratory people of the era loved,

> While Mr. Benson has wealth, wealth won by toil and thrift, and certain fortuitous circumstance, we of Oregon are here to honor the man, not his money. . . . He has interested himself in things great and good for Oregon, and it is evident that he has regarded his wealth as a public trust rather than a purely selfish possession. Mr. Benson was selected as Oregon's most notable citizen because of the greatness of his soul, the extent of his good works, and the fact that he has promoted human brotherhood. He is worthy of the honor Oregon has

paid him and worthy of all the honor this greatest of expositions can give him.

Benson himself seemed proud but rather ill at ease with all this laudatory language. The *San Francisco Chronicle* described Benson as a "mild little Norwegian" who looked "diffident." The article went on to claim he had arrived from Norway wearing wooden shoes. In response to Withycombe's speech and the three cheers that followed, he said simply, "Anything I may have done for the state was a pleasure to me, in fact, a duty I owed to the state which has done so much for me." Other festivities honoring Benson included a parade of more than twenty decorated cars from the St. Francis Hotel to the fair site in the Marina District, and a band playing "Hail the Conquering Hero." Other speakers included a representative of California Governor Hiram Johnson and a Portland attorney named John F. Logan who was the Oregon "commissioner" for the exposition. The ceremony, held at the Exposition's Court of Abundance, was followed by a reception at the Palace of Transportation, which featured a panorama of the Columbia River Highway, and then a luncheon at the Oregon Pavilion, hosted by Logan. A decade or so later, Benson and Logan would form another connection as Benson's youngest son Chester married Logan's daughter Dorothy.

SIMON BENSON

Benson, fourth from left, surrounded by dignitaries as he is named "Oregon's Notable Citizen" at the Panama-Pacific International Exposition. (Benson family collection)

*

Back in Oregon, as Benson continued to promote construction of the Columbia River Highway and other roads throughout Oregon, he had a final significant contribution he wanted to make to his home city of Portland. Despite his great business and financial success, Benson was keenly aware of the limits of his own education, and as proud as he was of the contributions of his son Amos to the family businesses and to the Columbia River Highway, he also felt disappointment that Amos had never gone further in his schooling. Benson realized as well how quickly technology was developing and he recognized the need for a better-educated workforce; therefore, he decided Portland needed a high school that would focus on teaching modern technical skills. On 31 July 1915, he told the Portland School District Board of Directors he wanted to donate one hundred thousand dollars for "the purpose of building the first unit of a School of Trades, upon condition that the District contract to expend at least $100,000 during the year 1916, in the construction of a second unit to the school." The board accepted his offer with gratitude and alacrity.

Such a school did already exist in Portland: the Portland School of Trades had opened in 1908 with the mission to give "boys who wished to enter a trade a better opportunity than do shops and factories of the present time." Starting the following year, girls were allowed to attend, taking classes in "sewing, cooking, millinery, and homemaking." In 1913, the girls' program was moved to a different location. However, the school Benson proposed would be considerably larger and more ambitious.

Benson believed more schools should offer education in practical, real-world skills. He agreed with Stewart Holbrook, who once said, "Many able housewives, plumbers, and electricians have been ruined by Greek and

Latin piped into them in their early lives." Benson believed that a young man should learn a trade. (Like so many of his contemporaries, apparently including Holbrook, he was not quite so concerned about women.) He embodied old-fashioned conservative values: good workers were good for business, of course, but they were also good for the country and its moral standing, and the forces of Bolshevism could not make inroads. In the 1920s, he said:

> The reason I gave a hundred thousand dollars toward establishing the Benson Polytechnic School was to give our boys a chance to learn trades and become self-supporting, self-respecting citizens. If a man has a trade, he can earn money. This means he is apt to get married and own a home. The forces of discontent can make no converts among workmen who own homes and have family ties. We need fewer men who are looking for white-collar jobs. I have no interest in a man who is unwilling to sweat. Too many applied to me for work who were unwilling to get calluses on their hands. What we need is producers, both in the city and on the farm, men who are willing to work. Teach more of our boys a trade, teach more of our girls to cook, to

raise babies and to be homemakers, and there will be less industrial unrest. The test of an educational institution should be, "Is it turning out good citizens? Will its graduates become producers or parasites? Will they be an asset or a liability to a community? Has the school or college a real part in the upbuilding of the community and the state?" As I see it, the only cure for industrial unrest is for all of us, employers and employees, to deal justly with our fellow men. Right is right and wrong is wrong, irrespective of the size of your bank balance or the kind of clothes you wear.

Benson Polytechnic High School in Portland. (Photo by author)

Possibly the most important words in this quote are "industrial unrest." It is necessary to keep in mind that when Benson said this the Russian Revolution had only recently occurred, and workers around the United States were restless and dissatisfied. This was the era of the radical Industrial Workers of the World – the Wobblies – and anarchist bombings. The Wobblies had made especially strong inroads in the logging industry, especially in the Pacific Northwest; loggers in many camps faced horrific working conditions. Though the surviving evidence suggests that Benson treated his workers well, and of course he had stopped participating in the industry some years before, he would not have been sympathetic to the demands of people he would have seen as radicals. Benson himself believed in and in fact embodied the notion of the immigrant boy who came to America and made good by the sweat of his brow. He had retired from the logging and lumber industry, but he deeply believed in supporting his adoptive country and the values by which he felt he had succeeded the best way he knew how.

Benson Polytechnic High School opened its doors in time for the start of the 1917 school year; however, its first "class" consisted not of ambitious students but of soldiers about to ship off to World War I. The federal government had taken over the building for use as a training base and called its program "Soldiers of Industry." Even after the war's end, the government may have continued to use Benson Tech: in 1919 it appears about fifty wounded veterans were sent there for retraining. It would serve as "the state's major war industry training center" during World War II as well. The school took in its first class of regular students in 1919. For some years after, Benson would make loans and grants to low-income students he found especially "worthy."

Benson Tech continues today as one of the finest Portland public high schools. As well as taking the standard high school curriculum, students may focus on fields like Industrial, Engineering, or Communications Technology, or Health Occupations. It has a higher graduation rate than other Portland high schools and it is the only Portland high school that graduates more minority students than white ones. One might say that the school is his greatest legacy, greater even than the highway, and with the advent of new technologies it continues to excel in ways Benson himself might not have foreseen.

*

After the highway project ended, Benson continued to campaign for good roads in Oregon. He supported the efforts of the state – which had now started providing major highway funding – to build the Pacific Highway through Oregon, connecting it with roads in California and Washington. This would be known as U.S. Highway 99. He also wanted a parallel road built up the center of the state. This would allow tourists to make a great circle through Oregon, driving in one direction past Crater Lake, through the gorge, then to Portland and down through the Willamette Valley and beyond. U.S. Highway 97 would be the second highway.

In 1921, Benson completed construction of the Columbia Gorge Hotel in Hood River, his final gift to the scenic highway. The twenty-three-acre property had been the site of the Wau-Gwin-Gwin Hotel, which Benson bought from owner Robert Rand for thirty-five thousand dollars. The property's name derives from the local Native American word for "rushing water." A lovely waterfall on the property flows from a spot near the hotel building and drops more than two hundred feet into the Columbia River. Benson had the old, rustic hotel torn down and oversaw construction in its place of a grand mission-style structure which guests and admirers soon came to call "the Waldorf of the West" for its beauty and elegance. The construction cost some three hundred thousand dollars. Guests who stayed there included Presidents Roosevelt and Coolidge, and actors Myrna Loy, Jane Powell, and Shirley Temple. Rudolph Valentino found it a particularly comfortable hideaway. Every one of the forty-eight rooms had private baths (at a time when this was still a sign of considerable luxury) and the main dining room could accommodate six hundred guests. Benson brought his gifted chef Henry Thiele, whose ability James Beard so admired, from the Benson Hotel in Portland to oversee the kitchen; he then also made Thiele the hotel's first manager. The grounds were decorated with local trees, small streams, rock gardens, tennis courts, a croquet ground, a little golf course, and walking paths. Some of the same Italian stonemasons who had previously worked at Maryhill and on the Scenic Columbia River Highway helped to decorate the grounds with retaining walls and arched bridges in the same style. Atop the hotel stands a one-hundred-foot tower offering a commanding twenty-five-mile view up and down the Columbia River.

SIMON BENSON

*Postcard of the Columbia Gorge Hotel.
(Wikimedia photo)*

Benson said his motivation for building the hotel was in keeping with the spirit in which he so enthusiastically sponsored the Scenic Columbia River Highway: "My main thought is not a profit-making enterprise, but to express my ideas of what a tourist hotel ought to be as an adjunct to highway development and tourist attraction. It is not only essential to make our valleys and mountains accessible by good highways, but it is further necessary to capitalize them by pleasant and comfortable hotels." While the highway was certainly an engineering marvel, in the relatively primitive cars of the day, such as Ford's Model T, the drive from Portland to Hood River would still take the better part of a day, especially with stops at Vista House, Multnomah Falls, and other sites. The Columbia Gorge Hotel would prove popular as an overnight stop, and lucrative for Benson, especially as other highways would be built connecting Hood River to other scenic areas: Highway 35 heads south from there through what is now called the "Fruit Loop," a scenic area of apple and pear orchards, then over the shoulder of Mt. Hood, Oregon's highest peak, then connects to Highway 26 and the historical Timberline Lodge with its year-round skiing, and finally back to Portland.

    Benson seemed genuinely happy to donate money, time, and energy to his projects to make the Columbia Gorge beautiful and accessible, but he was certainly willing to make money from them too. As the mining magnate Cecil Rhodes once said, "Pure philanthropy is all very well in its way, but philanthropy plus five percent is a good deal better." Just as he sold his interests in his lumber and logging business and in the Benson Hotel, he soon gave up control of the Columbia Gorge Hotel. He may have taken a loss on the project, a rare failure for such a consummate businessman. It went bankrupt in 1930, during the Depression, and has gone through various owners with varying success ever since.

SIMON BENSON

Benson may have had another motive for building a hotel in Hood River: it was the home of Mrs. Harriet King. A widow and native Oregonian, since her previous husband's death she had overseen her own orchards and business interests. She also had been "instrumental in organizing activities in interests of highway improvement in the Hood River district." Clearly, she shared some of Benson's main interests and perhaps character traits as well. One contemporary news article describes her as "a woman of great charm of personality and of distinguished appearance." Benson had divorced his second wife, Pamelia, some time around 1910, and now he felt ready for a third marriage. The couple wed in 1920 at the Benson Hotel, after a quite brief engagement – it was only formally announced a few days before the wedding – while the Columbia Gorge Hotel was still under construction. They honeymooned at the famous Hotel Del Monte Lodge on California's Monterey Peninsula; it was a favorite getaway spot for presidents, business titans, and celebrities. Its twenty thousand acres included the lands of the Pebble Beach Golf Course. A serious fire would destroy the hotel in 1924, and one wonders if some of the inspiration for the rebuilt structure, opened in 1926, came from the Spanish mission-style construction of the Columbia Gorge Hotel.

SIMON BENSON

From the Monterey Peninsula the couple continued on to Long Beach, California, where Benson had begun spending his winters in recent years.

In his late sixties, Simon Benson felt ready to leave Oregon permanently, for all that he loved it. Warmer weather and other business interests in Southern California now beckoned. His oldest son Amos, now with several children of his own, had overseen selling off the last of the Benson logging and lumber interests and now lived in Los Angeles, where he handled his father's interests. Benson's younger son Chester would soon follow along with his wife Dorothy, and he would have children of his own there. (Chester's son Gilbert Thomas, known as Tom, would spend most of his life in Portland and would consider it a matter of great embarrassment that he had been born in Los Angeles. This is not an unusual attitude for long-time Oregonians.) Sadly, Simon Benson's middle son, Gilbert Thereon Benson, would die on 16 April 1928, age only thirty-one, of sepsis. While he never had the opportunity to start a family of his own, Gilbert Thereon Benson left behind an interesting legacy: he wrote a book entitled *The Trees and Shrubs of Western Oregon*. Stanford University, his alma mater, published it after his death, and it was well received as a serious work of botanical scholarship.

SIMON BENSON

Benson and his new wife spent a couple more years alternating between Portland and Long Beach. He continues to appear frequently in news articles in Portland and other Oregon cities through the summer of 1922. But the number of times he is mentioned quickly tapers off. He would still visit from time to time: in 1924 he was the guest of honor at a testimonial dinner at which he was presented with a "medallion in sculpture" to honor his service to the city of Portland and the state of Oregon. The dinner was held "under the auspices of the Knights of Electra and sponsored by the Portland Chamber of Commerce." In another example of the era's florid oratory, former Oregon Governor Ben Olcott said,

> Oregon owes Simon Benson a heavy debt of gratitude for the invaluable services which he has rendered. He is one of our greatest and best citizens and, as Oregonians know, his services to the state have by no means been confined to what he has done in the way of highway development. But his efforts along that line alone will make him forever remembered by the people of the state. He has been in a large measure one of the foremost pioneers in the movement to pull Oregon out of the mud. His own money, his time, his services, all have been at

the command of the people of the state in this enormous undertaking, and he has given of them unstintedly [sic]. Mr. Benson has reared for himself in the hearts of the people of Oregon an enduring monument, and every man, woman and child in the state should have a just appreciation of his splendid services so freely given.

An article on taxes from 1925 identifies Benson as "reputed to be the wealthiest resident of Oregon." He is said to have paid about three hundred thirty dollars in federal taxes that year. By 1928, however, Benson is being referred to as a "former Oregonian"; by this time, he had decided to make Southern California his full-time home. However, he did retain some connections to Oregon, albeit at arm's length. In 1928, he ceremonially planted a Port Orford cedar tree in a botanical garden near Los Angeles. He did this "on behalf of the state of Oregon" for a display presenting a tree from each state in the Union.

Benson determined that Long Beach would not do as a place for permanent residence. The city had started to change dramatically in recent years, especially after the discovery of oil there in 1921. It became more and more a city of oil wells and refineries, factories, port facilities, and a U.S. Navy base. Benson decided he wanted to live in a more refined environment, and the place he chose was about as far up the scale as one could go in the greater Los Angeles area. He

Benson with a friend. (Benson family collection)

built a sumptuous home on the corner of Sunset Boulevard and Mountain Drive in Beverly Hills. His daughter Alice Benson Allen describes it as a "'show place' of Spanish architecture located on many landscaped acres, at the rear of which was a grove of Eucalyptus trees with a small stream running through." While Benson was happy in the more salubrious climate of Southern California, he clearly still remembered and appreciated Oregon's beauty: when someone remarked on the attractiveness of the grove of eucalyptus trees in his yard, Benson responded, "Did you ever see a Douglas Fir forest in Oregon?"

SIMON BENSON

During the mid-1930s, Benson's third marriage ended. Like his marriage to Pamelia which ended in the 1900s, his marriage to Harriet foundered on the rocks of irreconcilable differences – or "conflicting interests," as his daughter says. She appears to have been more interested in moving in the "high society" circles of Southern California than he was. Although attitudes had started to change by the 1930s, many people in the early twentieth century considered divorce to be embarrassing or even scandalous. It would not be a decision Benson would take lightly. Benson family lore tells of a letter hidden among Pamelia's effects, found by her descendants many years after her death. The letter came from a Portland doctor who asserted that he had examined Mrs. Benson and found her to be entirely of sound mind. A letter like this would serve as an "insurance policy" for a well-to-do woman of the era, preventing her husband from declaring her insane and sending her to an asylum until an easy and scandal-free divorce was granted. The fact that Benson gave Pamelia a generous settlement suggests her letter had the desired effect. Interestingly, some twenty years after the divorce, Pamelia had herself listed as Simon Benson's "widow" in a Portland city directory. Since Harriet was already independently fairly wealthy before she married Simon

Benson, he may not have needed to worry about having to make a significant financial settlement with her. Their marriage being childless and taking place in Beverly Hills, home of open-minded movie stars who married and divorced relatively casually, would also contribute to the dissolution of the Bensons' marriage being free of any scandal or negative talk.

After her father's divorce, Alice Benson Allen moved to Los Angeles with her family in 1936 to help care for him. Benson built for the Allen family a large house, something like eight thousand square feet on two stories. It contained four large bedrooms, an enormous living room and dining area, a double garage, and quarters for a live-in maid. According to a relative of Benson's who visited in 1930, Benson's mansion had about forty rooms.

Newly single again, Benson stayed on in his new home in Beverly Hills. He was no longer married, but he was far from alone. He employed two male servants, a cook, and a gardener. His two surviving sons lived nearby with their families. Even in his eighties, Benson found it impossible to truly retire and live a life of luxury and ease: "His restless disposition led him gradually back into active business," Alice Benson Allen says. He began to buy vacant parcels of land, subdivide them, and sell them at a profit. He started managing properties in and around Beverly Hills and along Santa Monica Boulevard, sometimes working with people in the film industry. He included actor Wallace Beery and director and screenwriter King Vidor among his circle of friends and acquaintances. Benson also bought properties to develop himself, building stores and gas stations which he leased to other people to run. Late in his eighties he even began talking about returning to the lumber business, this time in South America, but nothing came of it. Despite his wealth and reputation for philanthropy, Benson did not give money to just anyone. Late in the Great Depression – which of course affected much of the world, not just the United States – he received a letter from one of the leading citizens of Østre Gausdal, his hometown in Norway. In broken English, the writer, John (Johan) Kankrud, told Benson of his own experience as a logger in Oregon, and his return to Østre Gausdal in his later years where he had become a member of the Herredstyret or Town Council. He asked Benson, the proverbial local boy who went to America and made good, if he might donate some money for a senior center in the town, which had fallen on hard financial times. He emphasized how grateful and proud the town's elderly people would be, and how they would be happy to name the center in his honor: The Benson Home for Old People in Østre Gausdal, or if he preferred, Simon Benson's Mother and Fathers Home for Old People in Østre Gausdal. Benson's response seems highly disingenuous: he said the Stock Market Crash of 1929 had left him "hit pretty hard financially," his stocks and bonds had gone to "almost nothing" and not returned. This from the millionaire in his forty-room mansion in Beverly Hills. One wonders if this was the response of an old man growing increasingly miserly, or if he truly wanted to turn his back on his Norwegian roots and devote himself purely to his new identity in his new country. Either way, it clouds the picture of him that he had cultivated for himself as a great and generous benefactor.

SIMON BENSON

Last photo of Simon Benson. (Photo courtesy of the Oregon Historical Society)

Simon Benson died of heart failure on 5 August 1942, just a few weeks short of his ninety-first birthday. Alice Benson Allen says he loved to reminisce about his life in Oregon and she suggests that until the end his mind stayed clear and sharp. His body was brought to Portland and buried at River View Cemetery. Since all but one of Benson's surviving children were products of his marriage to Esther Searle, her body was exhumed from its grave in Colfax, Washington, and brought to Portland to lie beside her husband's. The plot features a large central monument with the graves of Simon, Esther, and each of Simon's children surrounding it. Pamelia Benson was buried at River View also after her death in 1945, but in a separate plot some distance away. One of Pamelia and Simon's grandchildren, Gilbert Thomas Benson, and his wife, are also buried near her as the main Benson plot is full.

The *Oregonian* newspaper remembered Benson for his "imaginative foresight" in its front-page obituary. The obituary offers a fairly complete biographical sketch, though it contains a good number of errors starting with his age – the paper said he was 89 – and the location of his birth: near someplace called "Lillibraner," Norway, a location that does not exist. After quietly spending most of the last twenty years of his life in California, it appears that Portland and Oregon would soon start to forget Simon Benson. Other Oregon newspapers gave his death only the most minimal coverage. However, Benson would receive one final honor less than a year after his death. With World War II raging, Portland and nearby Vancouver, Washington, became major centers for shipbuilding. Portland had several shipyards, and Henry Kaiser had built one in

SIMON BENSON

Vancouver. On 30 May 1943, the keel was laid down at the Oregon Shipbuilding Corporation for a liberty ship named the S.S. *Simon Benson*. The liberty ships were among the nation's great accomplishments of the war, built cheaply and very quickly, but in enormous numbers to carry troops and supplies to every theater of the war. More than two thousand seven hundred liberty ships were built, each able to carry several thousand tons of cargo. Mirroring her namesake's efficiency, the *Simon Benson* was launched just three weeks after her keel was laid, on 19 June 1943. Later, even this construction speed would be eclipsed: at the height of production, shipyards managed to turn out a liberty ship in about ten days. After the war, like most liberty ships the *Simon Benson* was sold into private hands, where she continued in service for more than twenty years before finally being scrapped in the late 1960s.

Benson's name lives on today attached to various recognizable and popular locations; the Benson Bubblers, the Benson Hotel, Benson Polytechnic High School, Benson State Recreation Area keep his name highly visible to Portlanders and visitors to the Northwest. But the man himself and much of his legacy seem to have been left behind. Many Portlanders would be hard-pressed to identify the person whose name is on all those things; many do not even realize they are all named for the same person. As Simon Benson himself might have said, it's time to change that. More than his name deserves to be remembered.

Afterword

Simon Benson was my great-grandfather. I was given the first name of my grandfather, Simon's youngest son Chester. I never knew Simon; he died years before I was born. In fact, I barely even really knew my grandfather since he died when I was just twelve years old, about the same age as my father when Simon died. The people who knew Simon personally and well are long gone. This means I have had to learn almost everything about him for this book through researching books and articles and websites, not interviews. Aside from one or two family stories, which I have identified as such, everything here comes from published sources. Why is this important to mention? There has only been one other full-length biography of Simon Benson, written by his daughter Alice more than fifty years ago. That book reads like a *hagiography* – a biography of a saint. While it is reasonably complete, its goal is more to tell his story uncritically, with nothing but praise. I set out on this project with the idea of rectifying that situation. I have used information from that previous book, especially for personal stories about Simon and his family, but whenever possible I verified the information with other sources. After half a century, I felt it was time to write a book that might really examine the man himself, not positively or negatively, but honestly.

Whether I have succeeded in realizing that goal is up to you, the reader, to decide.

As a child, I vaguely knew my great-grandfather had been someone important in the forestry industry. As I got older, I picked up more bits of information: that he was a noted philanthropist in Portland and Oregon, that a local high school and a nice hotel and some drinking fountains bore his name. But my father was curiously uninterested in his family's history and did not tell me much about Simon or encourage me to develop an interest in him. Later still, he told me that in actuality he had a deeply cynical view of Simon. My father felt that Simon was only ever interested in making money, that even his philanthropic donations were designed to use a minimal outlay of cash in order to gain a maximum amount of publicity and fame. After my own research I do not fully agree with my father, but I can certainly say in this regard that Simon was very good at getting his money's worth.

So I grew up bearing the Benson name but with little understanding of what it meant. Only when I was well into my adulthood did I start to develop a serious interest of my own in Simon. I think my father's death in 2011 was what started me down the road to writing this book. Among his possessions were many family photos, mostly of his own life but some of his own father's childhood and a few of Simon. Finding those got me interested in looking again at Alice Benson Allen's book, *Simon Benson: Northwest Lumber King*, and that in turn got me thinking about how useful it would be to have a better book about Simon and his life.

The question that kept coming into my mind as I started researching and writing about him and thinking about my father's opinion, was quite simple: *Would I have liked Simon Benson?* Would I have found him enjoyable company? Would it be fun to spend time with him? The answer, after several years of thought and research, is that I'm still not sure, but I doubt it. On one hand, Simon must have had remarkable charisma. He fell in love with a beautiful and quite young girl from a higher social status and, despite having few serious prospects, convinced her parents to let him marry her. He was always able to find people who treated him well and gave him good jobs and extended credit when he needed it. Almost immediately after he arrived in Oregon, as he took a boat from Portland to the closest logging areas in order to look for work, someone hired him as foreman of a logging crew, making more money than he ever had before. After he went into business for himself as an independent timber operator, he also inspired trust in the businessmen from whom he needed credit to keep his operations running. He persuaded them to extend his due dates. He always paid his debts, although sometimes it took him a while.

He also must have been extremely intelligent. He had little formal schooling and arrived in America in his teens not able to speak a word of English. Yet he persevered, and with the help of his first American employer he mastered the language – one of the most difficult in the world – with stunning speed. He understood all aspects of his chosen occupation and performed them with great competence. Later in his career, he showed an innate grasp of engineering, succeeding in highly technical operations in locations where others had failed: adopting the use of steam donkeys, building railroads in the muddy mountains of the Coast Range, and of course his crowning achievement, building great oceangoing log rafts.

Another admirable quality he demonstrated was vision, or foresight: he repeatedly worked to prepare for and support what he saw as important future trends. His early adoption of technology in logging illustrates this. He knew it was coming, and that it would revolutionize his industry. He wanted to be one of the great influencers in that revolution and achieve great success for himself in the process. Even more telling in regard to his vision was his recognition of the coming of the automobile, and specifically the influence it would have on the enormous growth of an industry that few envisioned in the early twentieth century: tourism. His construction of the Benson Hotel that still bears his name a century after he sold his interest in it, and his championing of roads that gave access to scenic parts of Oregon, demonstrate this foresight.

In her book, Alice Benson Allen asserts that Simon Benson was a dreamer: even as a child in Norway, she says, he would tell people about how rich and successful he would become. On hearing this, adults would shake their heads and accuse him of "building air castles." Benson made this claim himself. Yet in spite of this rather romantic image, in reality the immediate impression Simon Benson has left behind is largely of an ambitious but hard-headed and even cold-blooded man who was deeply preoccupied by money. In the 1920s a short autobiography by him appeared. In just a few pages he summarizes his life from the beginning until his retirement. Two things stand out about this little essay. First, he seems to recall exactly how much money he made or lost at every moment throughout his life. He remembers the value of his parents' small landholding in Norway, and how much money his father made as a day laborer. He remembers the fare his brother paid for bringing each family member to America – fifty-three dollars – and how soon he paid his own fare back. He mentions that he paid thirty dollars a month to the man he hired to assist him in his first independent logging operation. His memory seems uncanny but also perhaps somewhat obsessive in his emphasis on money. His daughter Alice also mentions that while he loved to play pinochle, he was not a fun opponent because he so quickly memorized all the cards and thus always won; he always had to be on top of the numbers, no matter what he was doing.

His obsession with money seems excessive. Yes, one can excuse such financial concerns in a person who grew up poor. And yes, he worked and lived the American dream, but his emphasis on money stands in marked contrast to what is missing from this autobiography: emotion. Simon comes across as almost entirely unsentimental. He barely mentions his parents, except to talk about the work they did, and he says virtually nothing about his siblings. Only when his wife dies does he say anything about how he felt, and even that he puts into the context of money. Paying the doctor and funeral expenses after her death left him without any funds. "I was used to being broke, so I didn't mind it," he says, "but losing my partner, that was a heavy blow, one that was very hard to recover from." That is the only tender, sentimental moment in the essay's several thousand words. In the entire piece, he only names his oldest son Amos once and never even mentions his two daughters, or the second wife he married a few years later, or the two more sons he had with her, or the death of one of those later sons. Either he apparently believed that in general, sentiment was not something to share, or else he simply did not feel it much. He says of himself, "I am pretty hard-headed in spite of my being accused of being a dreamer and a visionary." Thus, he directly contradicts his daughter's rose-colored vision of him.

Simon held deeply conservative views of a kind that were not uncommon among businessmen of his era. He founded Benson Polytechnic High School because he believed in the vital importance of learning a trade. "If a man has a trade that means he can earn money," he said.

"This means that he is apt to get married and own a home. The forces of discontent can make no convert among workmen who own homes and have family ties." At a time when American business leaders feared "industrial unrest" from anarchists and communists, Simon did his best to prevent it. He wanted no part of unions or other efforts no reform industry in ways that might cost him money, although he did recognize that the changing country might someday elect a "labor president"; one imagines he hoped if that moment did come, it would be far in the future. Even his dislike of liquor was rooted in its financial costs: he "noticed for years how much liquor cost me in the decreased efficiency of the men in my logging camps and sawmills." Liquor also caused accidents which he found "annoying and expensive," and brought poverty to some of his workers and their families.

One also needs to recognize the environmental and aesthetic effects of Benson's chosen industry. There are basically two kinds of logging. One is selective cutting, or "thinning," in which a crew will only cut a limited number of trees in a given area. The benefit of this is that it causes less harm to the environment, protecting animal and plant species by allowing shade to cover fragile species and keeping water in rivers and streams cleaner and cooler. The alternative is called "clearcutting," and as its name suggests, it involves cutting down virtually all the trees in an area. This is harder on the environment: it eliminates habitat for plants and animals and allows streams to become muddy and warmer from direct sunlight; this can harm spawning grounds for the salmon for which the Pacific Northwest is famous. The benefit of clearcutting is that it is highly efficient and cost effective, far more so than selective logging.

Lumbermen like Simon Benson would choose clearcutting every time. He would have seen the forest as a source of money, and given little thought to its beauty. The forests of the Oregon Coast Range may have seemed nearly infinite, but Benson had seen the industry in Wisconsin, so he would have known better. The desire for wealth over all else would have been held in common by all the lumber operators of his era and for years after, fitting in with their conservative values. But there were others who did find clearcutting shocking: in 1937, Presideent Franklin D. Roosevelt toured the Olympic Peninsula and saw an enormous clearcut. Although he had just applauded a logging demonstration the day before, he was so shocked and disgusted by the scene, he said, "I hope the son of a bitch who logged that is roasting in hell."

SIMON BENSON

For much of the twentieth century, logging operations tried to keep clearcutting hidden from the general public. Highways through the forests would have a hundred yards or so of uncut trees on either side so the clearcutting remained invisible. More recently, those areas have been cut too – so much timber so obviously present was too much of a temptation. However, modern laws in Oregon require the logging companies promptly to replant their clearcut areas. The trees growing now likely will not be left long enough to replace the old-growth timber of the past, but at least the forests are being treated as a renewable resource.

As I mention in Chapter 7 of this book, during the Great Depression, when Simon was living in luxurious retirement in Southern California, he received a letter from one of the leading citizens of his hometown back in Norway. The writer happened to be an emigrant himself: he had come to America and worked as a logger in one of Benson's operations, then returned home to Norway for his retirement. Now the town was feeling the financial pinch just like everyone else in the world, he said, but they desperately needed a new senior center for the elderly people there. Everyone back home remembered Simon fondly as the local boy who had gone to America and made good. Could he perhaps find it in his heart to donate some money for the new center? Simon said no. He was feeling a little short of money, said the millionaire from his Beverly Hills mansion.

Why did he refuse? He could certainly have afforded it, and he was famous for his philanthropy. One possibility might be that he considered himself an American now, and he wanted to put his foreign roots behind him. Perhaps he just did not care about those people so far away. Perhaps he had grown miserly in his old age. Whatever the reason, to me it shows Simon in a negative light. Perhaps he just could not find any self-interest in it, as my father might have said. For all his talk about lifting people up, and his previous successful efforts at doing so, this time he refused without offering a legitimate explanation but only a lie.

Simon's singular focus on finances, costs, profits sometimes seems off-putting. It makes me understand my father's cynicism; it would be nice to find just one more statement from him saying something tender, caring, or funny – something that shows some feeling, some emotion. Alice describes her father as handsome: slim, about six feet tall, "with light brown hair and piercing blue eyes." He had a sense of humor, she says, and was "fun to be with." But I wish I could find an example of that. One can only see him smile in one or two of the hundreds of photos I have seen of him. Most of the time he appears serious, even dour.

I believe Simon is worthy of profound respect. He could indeed serve as the prototype of the American Dream: he was the poor immigrant boy who came to America, worked hard, and enjoyed huge success beyond his wildest dreams. He was an outstanding logger, an excellent amateur engineer, and a shrewd businessman. His social and political views were very conservative by today's standards, and I personally do not agree with all of them, but they were entirely in line with others in positions similar to his. He had amazing prescience: a talent for seeing what the future would hold and making for himself an important role in it. He clearly was highly charismatic. He gave generously to his adopted city and state, and if there was an element of self-interest in it, that is not so hard to understand.

But would I like him? Of that I'm still unsure. You, the reader, will have to make your own decisions.

Bibliography

Author's Note

Buckley, Camille. "How Did Iceland Become a Nation with No Surnames?" *Culture Trip*, 12 April 2018, https://theculturetrip.com/europe/iceland/articles/how-did-iceland-become-a-nation-with-no-surnames/

"Census Districts Summary: 1865 Census for Gausdal." *Digital Archive*, Norwegian National Archive, 22 July 2009, https://www.digitalarkivet.no/en/source/38064

"The History of Simon Benson and His House." *Portland State University Alumni Association*, 2020, https://www.pdx.edu/alumni/simon-benson-house

Lockley, Fred. *History of the Columbia River Valley from The Dalles to the Sea*, Vol. 2, S.J. Clarke, 1928. https://babel.hathitrust.org/cgi/pt?id=mdp.39015021226439;view=1up;seq=7

Nedrebø, Yngve. "How to Trace Your Ancestors in Norway." *Digital Archives,* Royal Norwegian

Ministry of Foreign Affairs, 2017, https://d.docs.live.net/64b15bd27fdc753a/Desktop/New%20Ideas/Simon%20Benson/Book/Complete/Newer%20Complete%202022/Author's%20Note%20Notes%20and%20Bib%2021723.docx

"Simon Benson: 1851-1942." *The Oregon History Project*, Oregon Historical Society, 19 Sept. 2019, https://oregonhistoryproject.org/articles/biographies/simon-benson-biography/#.Xs6xXkBFyUk

Unander, Sig. "Building Air Castles: Simon Benson's Lasting Oregon Legacy." *1859: Oregon's Magazine*, 24 April 2018, pp. 82-87, https://1859oregonmagazine.com/think-oregon/history/oregon-history-simon-bensons-legacy/

White, William Scott. "Simon Benson (1851-1942)." *Inclusity*, 15 April 2020, https://www.inclusity.com/simon-benson-1851-1942/

Chapter 1

"19th-Century Immigration and Growth." *Wisconsin Historical Society*, 2018, https://www.wisconsinhistory.org/Records/Article/CS3668

Alchin, Linda. "Norwegian Immigration to America." *U.S. Immigration*, 1 Jan. 2018, http://www.emmigration.info/norwegian-immigration-to-america.htm

Allen, Alice Benson. *Simon Benson: Northwest Lumber King*. Binfords and Mort, 1971,

"The Amazing History of Logging in the United States." *Wood Splitters Direct*, https://www.woodsplitterdirect.com/the-amazing-history-of-logging-in-the-united-states/. Accessed 26 May 2020.

"An 'American Letter' by Norwegian Immigrants." *Wisconsin Historical Society*, 2018, https://www.wisconsinhistory.org/Records/Article/CS3091

Ancestry.com. *U.S., Evangelical Lutheran Church in America Church Records, 1781-1969* [database online]. Lehi, UT, USA: Ancestry.com Operations, Inc., 2015.

---. *U.S., Find A Grave Index, 1600s-Current* [database online]. Provo, UT, USA: Ancestry.com Operations, Inc., 2012.

Anderson, David Allen. *The School System of Norway.* 1912. The State University of Iowa, Ph.D. dissertation. https://iro.uiowa.edu/esploro/outputs/doctoral/The-school-system-of-Norway/9983777051902771?institution=01IOWA_INST

Blegen, Theodore C., ed. "Behind the Scenes of Emigration: A Series of Letters from the 1840's by Johan R. Reierson." Translated by Carl O. Paulson and the Verdandi Study Club, *Norwegian-American Studies and Records*, vol. 14, 1944, *JSTOR.* https://www.jstor.org/stable/45220285

Borgos, Johan I. "Norwegian Farm Names." *Slekt & Historie (Ancestry and History)*, http://www.borgos.nndata.no/farms.htm. Accessed 30 May 2020.

Bryson, Bill. *Made in America*. Perennial, 2001.

"Church Book from Gausdal Parish, 1850-1861." *Digital Archive*, Norwegian National Archive, 2 Jan. 2007, https://www.digitalarkivet.no/en/source/8940

Dbug. "Peace, Potatoes, and Pox (Norwegian Emigration in the 1800s). *Daily Kos*, 10 September 2014, https://www.dailykos.com/stories/2014/9/10/1328867/-Peace-Potatoes-and-Pox-Norwegian-Emigration-in-the-1800s

"Ellis Island History." *The Statue of Liberty – Ellis Island*, 2020, https://www.libertyellisfoundation.org/ellis-island-history

Elmer, Jeffrey L. "Simon Benson." *Oregon Bios Project*, September 2006, http://jtenlen.drizzlehosting.com/ORBios/sbenson.html

Fitch, Catherine A., and Steven Ruggles. *Historical Trends in Marriage Formation, United States 1850-1990*. Department of History, University of Minnesota, http://users.hist.umn.edu/~ruggles/Articles/Fitch_and_Ruggles.pdf. Accessed 26 May 2020.

Halvorson, Arne. Historian in Gausdal, Norway. Personal letter to author. 31 January 2022.

Haukås, Åsta. "Metacognition in Language Learning and Teaching: An Overview." *Metacognition in Language Learning and Teaching*. Edited by Asta Haukas, Camilla Bjørke, and Magne Dypedahl. Routledge, 2018, *Google Books*, https://books.google.com/books?id=hWJgDwAAQBAJ&pg=PT122&dq=norwegian+similarity+english&hl=en&sa=X&ved=0ahUKEwih7o2HuJrjAhXLJzQIHdIrA3EQ6AEINTAC#v=onepage&q=norwegian%20similarity%20english&f=false

"Historical Ecology of the Upper Midwest." *U.S. Forest Service*, United States Department of Agriculture, 2006. https://www.nrs.fs.fed.us/fmg/nfmg/fm101/eco/p1_historical.html

"History of Logging." *History*, A & E Networks, 2018. https://www.history.co.uk/shows/ax-men/articles/history-of-logging

"Horrible Famine in Sweden and Norway." *Daily Alta California*, 14 Feb. 1868. *California Digital*

Newspaper Collection, UCR Center for Bibliographical Studies and Research, 2018. https://cdnc.ucr.edu/cgi-bin/cdnc?a=d&d=DAC18680214.2.5&e=-------en--20--1--txt-txIN--------1

"Immigration...Scandinavian: Introduction." *Library of Congress,* https://www.loc.gov/classroom-materials/immigration/scandinavian. Accessed 26 May 2020.

"Immigration...Scandinavian: The Norwegians." *Library of Congress*, https://www.loc.gov/classroom-materials/immigration/scandinavian/the-norwegians/ Accessed 26 May 2020.

"Jane L. Dalton: Facts and Events." *We Relate*, 24 June 2007, https://www.werelate.org/wiki/Person:Jane_Dalton_(2)

Lieberman, Sara. "Norwegian Population Growth in the 19th Century." *Economy and History*, Taylor & Francis Online, 23 May 2012, doi/abs/10.1080/00708852.1968.10418873

Lockley, Fred. *History of the Columbia River Valley from The Dalles to the Sea*, Vol. 2, S.J. Clarke, 1928, https://babel.hathitrust.org/cgi/pt?id=mdp.39015021226439;view=1up;seq=7

Merk, Frederick. *Economic History of Wisconsin During the Civil War Decade*, State Historical Society of Wisconsin, vol. 1, 1916.

Olsen, Dan. Descendant of Stina Bergersen. Email to author. 27 Jan. 2022

"Østre Gausdal Church." *Hafjell Resort*, 2018, https://www.hafjellresort.no/en/book/to-do/1575282/østre-gausdal-church/showdetails

"Paul Bunyan." *Wikipedia*, 29 Oct. 2018. https://en.wikipedia.org/wiki/Paul_Bunyan

Perry, Roy. "Simon Benson, Lumber King." *Columbia County History*, Columbia County Historical Society, vol. 16, 1977, pp. 26-28.

"Rise of Industrial America, 1876-1900: Immigration to the United States, 1851-1900." *The Library of Congress*, http://www.loc.gov/teachers/classroommaterials/pre

sentationsandactivities/presentations/timeline/risein d/immgnts/ . Accessed 25 May 2020.

"Simon Benson." *Find a Grave*, 8 Oct. 2001, https://www.findagrave.com/memorial/5833074/simon-benson

"Simon A Benson (Iversen)." *Geni*, 2021. https://geni.com/people/Simon-Benson/6000000020575067427

Voss, Don and Grace. *Footprints to America.* Unpublished history of Benson family, 2000.

White, William Scott. "Simon Benson (1851-1942)." *Inclusity*, 15 April 2020, https://www.inclusity.com/simon-benson-1851-1942/

Wilson, Colwick M. *Domestic Work in The United States of America: Past Perspectives and Future Directions*, https://www.academia.edu/32208627/Domestic_Work_in_The_United_States_of_America_Past_Perspectives_and_Future_Directions?pop_sutd=false. Accessed 20 May 2020.

"Wisconsin's Involvement in the Civil War." *Wisconsin Historical Society*, 2018.

https://www.wisconsinhistory.org/Records/Article/CS3355

Chapter 2

"A Brief Summary of Oregon Coast Range Geology, Geomorphology, Tectonics, and Climate." *Geology 4/510: Tectonic Geomorphology*, University of Oregon, https://dl.icdst.org/pdfs/files3/f860124fc748cc5317166e7b105d525f.pdf Accessed 27 January 2022.

Abbott, Carl. "Portland (Essay)." *The Oregon Encyclopedia*, Oregon Historical Society, 10 July 2019, https://oregonencyclopedia.org/articles/portland/#.Xpues0BFyUk

Allen, Alice Benson. *Simon Benson: Northwest Lumber King*. Binfords and Mort, 1971.

Ancestry.com. *U.S., Find A Grave Index, 1600s-Current* [database on-line]. Provo, UT, USA: Ancestry.com Operations, Inc., 2012.

Andrews, Alicia, and Kristen Kutara. "Oregon's Timber Harvests: 1849-2004." *Oregon Department of Forestry*, 2005, https://www.oregon.gov/ODF/Documents/Working Forests/oregonstimberharvests.pdf

Becker, Paula. "Colfax – Thumbnail History." *History Link*, 20 Sept. 2010, https://www.historylink.org/File/9580

Carey, Charles Henry. "Sylvester Farrell." *History of Oregon*, Oregon Bios. Project, 2005, http://jtenlen.drizzlehosting.com/ORBios/sfarrell1.txt

"City of Portland Annexation History." *PortlandOregon.gov*, https://www.portlandoregon.gov/cbo/article/433188 . Accessed 21 April 2020.

"Climate in Colfax, Washington." *Best Places*, Sperling's Best Places, https://www.bestplaces.net/climate/city/washington/colfax. Accessed 25 April 2020.

"Climate in Astoria, Oregon." *Best Places*, Sperling's Best Places, https://www.bestplaces.net/climate/city/oregon/astoria. Accessed 7 April 2020.

"Climate in Forks, Washington." *Best Places*, Sperling's Best Places, https://www.bestplaces.net/climate/city/washington/forks. Accessed 7 April 2020.

"Climate in St. Helens, Oregon." *Best Places*, Sperling's Best Places, https://www.bestplaces.net/climate/city/oregon/st._helens. Accessed 25 April 2020.

"Coast Ranges." *Encyclopaedia Britannica*, 2020, https://www.britannica.com/place/Coast-, Ranges

"Connect with Your Roots." *Oregon Forest Resources Institute*, 2020. https://oregonforests.org/node/19

Derks, Jacob. "Douglas Fir – Firing Up Foresters Since 1827." *EFI*, European Forest Institute, 17 Jan. 2019, https://resilience-blog.com/2019/01/17/douglas-fir-a-controversial-species-or-an-option-for-europe/

Dietrich, William. "Douglas Fir, Then and Now." *The Seattle Times*, 19 Mar. 2000, https://archive.seattletimes.com/archive/?date=20000319&slug=4010893

"Douglas Fir." *The National Wildlife Federation*, https://www.nwf.org/Educational-Resources/Wildlife-Guide/Plants-and-Fungi/Douglas-Fir. Accessed 8 April 2020.

"Douglas Fir – One of the Best Wood Species in the World." *Florida Lumber*, 20 Dec. 2017, https://floridalumber.com/blog/douglas-fir-one-of-the-best-wood-species-in-the-world/

"Douglas-fir." *Naturally: Wood*, Forestry Innovation Investment, 2020, https://www.naturallywood.com/forest-products-species/softwood-species/douglas-fir

"Earthquake Glossary: Ring of Fire." *USGS*, United States Geological Survey. https://earthquake.usgs.gov/learn/glossary/?term=Ring%20of%20Fire. Accessed 7 April 2020.

Entwistle, William. "Western Logging in the Early Days, from 1876 Onwards." *Skagit River Journal*, 15 Dec. 2008, http://www.skagitriverjournal.com/Logging/WAW/Log02-Entwistle1876.html

"Express Train Crosses the Nation in 83 Hours." *History*, A&E Television Networks, 28 July 2019, https://www.history.com/this-day-in-history/express-train-crosses-the-nation-in-83-hours

"Famous People Who Died of Tuberculosis." *The Famous People*, https://www.thefamouspeople.com/tuberculosis.php. Accessed 24 April 2020.

Federal Reserve Committee on Branch, Group, and Chain Banking. *Branch Banking in California*, 1932, https://fraser.stlouisfed.org/files/docs/historical/federal%20reserve%20history/frcom_br_gp_ch_banking/branch_banking_california.pdf

Frith, John. "History of Tuberculosis, Part I: Phthisis, Consumption, and the White Plague." *JMVH*, vol 22, no. 2 (June 2014). https://jmvh.org/article/history-of-tuberculosis-part-1-phthisis-consumption-and-the-white-plague/

Greeley, W.B. *Instructions for Appraising Stumpage on National Forests*, Forest Service, United States Department of Agriculture, 10 April 1922, https://books.google.com/books?id=LJBOAAAAMAAJ&pg=PA44&lpg=PA44&dq=50+cents+a+thous

and+stumpage&source=bl&ots=niaMbDbAsU&sig=ACfU3U16XMDMgR2-7Cfi_C-2qcz7l8F0WQ&hl=en&sa=X&ved=2ahUKEwj7wsTro4npAhVMrp4KHV6DBMAQ6AEwAHoECAoQAQ#v=onepage&q=50%20cents%20a%20thousand%20stumpage&f=false

Gurney, Darrell. "What Is the Surprising Meaning of the Odd Phrase 'Back Forty'?" *The Back Forty*, 2018. https://thebackforty.com/2017/02/28/what-is-the-surprising-meaning-of-the-odd-phrase-back-forty/

Hiskey, Daven. "Why Tuberculosis Was Called 'Consumption.'" *Today I Found Out*, 17 Mar. 2014, http://www.todayifoundout.com/index.php/2014/03/tuberculosis-called-consumption/

"History of Portland, Oregon." *United States History*, 2020, https://u-s-history.com/pages/h3903.html

Horn, Don. "Nancy Boggs Mullery (1833-1905)." *The Oregon Encyclopedia*, 9 August 2023, https://www.oregonencyclopedia.org/articles/boggs-nancy/

"How to Calculate Board Feet." *Woodworkers Source*, 2020, https://www.woodworkerssource.com/how-to-calculate-board-feet/board-foot-calculator.html

"How to Calculate Board Feet." *Woodworkers Source*, 2020, https://www.woodworkerssource.com/how-to-calculate-board-feet/board-foot-calculator.html

"Inflation Calculator." *DaveManuel.Com*, 3 May 2020, https://www.davemanuel.com/inflation-calculator.php

"Jane L. Dalton: Facts and Events." *We Relate*, 24 June 2007, https://www.werelate.org/wiki/Person:Jane_Dalton_(2)

Lang, Frank A. "Douglas-fir." *The Oregon Encyclopedia*, Oregon Historical Society, 4 June 2019, https://oregonencyclopedia.org/articles/douglas_fir/#.Xo1TFUBFyUk

Lockley, Fred. *History of the Columbia River Valley from The Dalles to the Sea*, Vol. 2, S.J. Clarke, 1928. https://babel.hathitrust.org/cgi/pt?id=mdp.39015021226439;view=1up;seq=7

Lundin, John W., and Stephen J. Lundin. "Stagecoach and Steamboat Travel in Washington's Early Days." *HistoryLink.org*, 21 Nov. 2012, https://www.historylink.org/File/10250.

McKittrick, Erin. "Temperate Rainforests of the Northern Pacific Coast." *Ground Truth Trekking*, 2011. http://www.groundtruthtrekking.org/Issues/Forestry/TemperateRainforests.html

McNeal, Wm. H. "History of Wasco County, Oregon." *Roots Web*, http://homepages.rootsweb.com/~westklic/howcoc2.html. Accessed 19 April 2020.

Murray, John F. "A Century of Tuberculosis." *American Journal of Respiratory and Critical Care Medicine*, vol 169, no. 11, ATS Journals, 2 Mar. 2004, https://www.atsjournals.org/doi/full/10.1164/rccm.200402-140OE

"Native American Uses of Utah Forest Trees." *Utah Forest Facts*, Utah State University Cooperative Extension, 2011. https://forestry.usu.edu/files/utah-forest-facts/native-american-uses-of-utah-forest-trees.pdf

Noss, Reed, et al. "Palouse Grasslands." *World Wildlife Fund*, 2020,

https://www.worldwildlife.org/ecoregions/na0813

"Old Clipping Tells of Benson Cabin; Contributions to Highway." *The Clatskanie Chief*, 13 July 2000: 2.

http://ctk.stparchive.com/Archive/CTK/CTK071320 00P02.php?tags=simon|benson.

"The Oregon Attitude." *BillMoyers.com*, 14 Nov. 1973, The Oregon Attitude | BillMoyers.com

"The Origin of the Word 'Tuberculosis.'" *Science Friday*, 24 Feb. 2012,

https://www.sciencefriday.com/segments/the-origin-of-the-word-tuberculosis/

Osborn, Liz. "Wettest Places in United States." *Current Results: Weather and Science Facts*, 2022.

https://www.currentresults.com/Weather-Extremes/US/wettest.php

"Pacific Coastal Rainforest of North America." *Alaska Coastal Rainforest Center*, University of Alaska Southeast,

https://www.uas.alaska.edu/acrc/_docs/data_publica

tions/factsheets/pacificcoastal.pdf. Accessed 7 April 2020.

Perry, Roy. "Simon Benson, Lumber King." *Columbia County History*, Columbia County Historical Society, vol. 16, 1977, pp. 26-28.

"Portland before It Was Portland: The Dark Side of the City of Roses." *Tropics of Meta*, 29 October 2015, https://tropicsofmeta.com/2015/10/29/portland-before-it-was-portland-the-dark-side-of-the-city-of-roses-2/

"Pseudotsuga Menziesii." *The Gymnosperm Database*, 2021. https://www.conifers.org/pi/Pseudotsuga_menziesii.php

"Quotes: Tom McCall: A Better Oregon." *The Oregon Historical Society*, 2021, https://www.ohs.org/education/curriculum/tom-mccall-better-oregon/quotes.cfm

"Reforestation Overview." *U.S. Forest Service*, United States Department of Agriculture, https://www.fs.fed.us/restoration/reforestation/overview.shtml. Accessed 27 January 2022

"Seeing the Forest for the Trees: Placing Washington's Forests in Historical Context." *Center for the Study of the Pacific Northwest*, University of Washington, https://www.washington.edu/uwired/outreach/cspn/Website/Classroom%20Materials/Curriculum%20Packets/Evergreen%20State/Section%20II.html. Accessed 17 April 2020

"Shipping Lines." *The Maritime Heritage Project*, 2018, https://www.maritimeheritage.org/ships/shippingLines.html

Sndr1235. "ELI5: Bull vs. Ox vs. Steer." *Reddit*, 2020, https://www.reddit.com/r/explainlikeimfive/comments/4uw5tp/eli5_bull_vs_ox_vs_steer/

Stelzer, Hank. "Forestry 101: Stumpage vs. Mill Delivered Price." *Green Horizons*, Agricultural Electronic Bulletin Board, University of Missouri Extension, vol. 15, no. 3, Summer 2011, http://agebb.missouri.edu/agforest/archives/v15n3/gh5.htm

"The Story Behind '40 Acres and a Mule." *Code Switch*, National Public Radio, 12 Jan. 2015, https://www.npr.org/sections/codeswitch/2015/01/12/376781165/the-story-behind-40-acres-and-a-mule

Szalay, Jessie. "Giant Sequoias and Redwoods: The Largest and Tallest Trees." *Live Science,* Future USA, Inc., 5 May 2017, https://www.livescience.com/39461-sequoias-redwood-trees.html

Table I: Population of the United States by States and Territories. "1880 Census Volume I: Statistics of the Population of the United States." *United States Census Bureau,* 1880 Census: Volume 1. Statistics of the Population of the United States. Accessed 19 June 2021

Thompson, Scott. "Lumberjack Tools of the 1800s." *The Classroom,* Leaf Group, Ltd., 17 May 2019, https://www.theclassroom.com/lumberjack-tools-of-the-1800s-12082940.html

Toll, William. "Early Portland." *The Oregon History Project.* Oregon Historical Society, 18 Sept. 2019, https://oregonhistoryproject.org/narratives/commerce-climate-and-community-a-history-of-portland-and-its-people/the-making-of-a-market-town/early-portland/#.XpuZtUBFyUk

"Tuberculosis (TB)." *Centers for Disease Control and Prevention,* U.S. Department of Health and Human

Services, 12 Dec. 2016,

https://www.cdc.gov/tb/worldtbday/history.htm

"Tutorial on the Public Land Survey Descriptions." *Wisconsin Department of Natural Resources*, https://dnr.wisconsin.gov/sites/default/files/topic/ForestManagement/PLSSTutorial.pdf

"What Are the Qualities of Fir Wood." *SFGate*, Hearst Newspapers, LLC, 2018, https://homeguides.sfgate.com/building-qualities-fir-wood-98839.html

"What Is the Origin of the Phrase 'Grease the Skids'?" *English Language and Usage*, 2022. https://english.stackexchange.com/questions/231468/what-is-the-origin-of-the-phrase-grease-the-skids

Chapter 3

Abbott, Carl. "Portland (Essay)." *The Oregon Encyclopedia*, Oregon Historical Society, 10 July 2019, https://oregonencyclopedia.org/articles/portland/#.Xs3YZUBFyUk

Allen, Alice Benson. *Simon Benson: Northwest Lumber King*. Binfords and Mort, 1971.

Ancestry.com. *Washington, U.S., Marriage Records, 1854-2013* [database on-line]. Provo, UT, USA: Ancestry.com Operations, Inc., 2012.

Ancestry.com. *Washington State and Territorial Censuses, 1857-1892*, Provo, UT, USA: Ancestry.com Operations Inc, 2006, https://search.ancestry.com/cgi-bin/sse.dll?indiv=1&dbid=1018&h=269655&tid=150985847&pid=172003763197&hid=1048024999438&usePUB=true&_phsrc=skh675&_phstart=default&usePUBJs=true

Ashworth, William B., Jr. "Scientist of the Day – Ephraim Shay." *Linda Hall Library,* 17 July 2019, https://www.lindahall.org/ephraim-shay/

"Benson Family Papers, 1889-1924." *Archives West*, Orbis Cascade Alliance, http://archiveswest.orbiscascade.org/ark:/80444/xv33120/pdf. Accessed 25 May 2020.

"The Benson Logging Company." *The Columbia County Historian Home Page*, http://www.twrps.com/history/columbia-river-logging/the-benson-logging-company/. Accessed 28 May 2020.

"A Brief History of the Museum." *Portland Art Museum*, https://portlandartmuseum.org/about/brief-history-museum/. Accessed 6 June 2020.

"Clark Kinsey & the Documentation of the Pacific Northwest Logging Industry: Camp Life." *University Libraries*, University of Washington, https://www.lib.washington.edu/specialcollections/collections/exhibits/Kinsey/camplife. Accessed 17 February 2024.

"The Clatskanie Historical Museum." *City of Clatskanie*, http://www.cityofclatskanie.com/aboutclatskanie/museum.html. Accessed 28 May 2020.

"Clatskanie's History." *Clatskanie, Oregon*, http://www.clatskanie.org/history.htm. Accessed 27 May 2020.

"Columbia County Logging Railroads." *VanNatta Logging History Museum of Northwest Oregon*, 11 Dec. 2012, http://www.vannattabros.com/histlog4.html

Conlin, Joseph R. "Old Boy, Did You Get Enough of Pie?: A Social History of Food in Logging Camps." *Journal of Forest History,* October 1979, pp. 164-

85, https://foresthistory.org/wp-content/uploads/2018/03/Conlin.pdf

Cox, Thomas R. "Lower Columbia Lumber Industry, 1880-93." *Oregon Historical Quarterly*, vol. 67, no. 2 (June 1966), pp. 160-78, *JSTOR*, https://www.jstor.org/stable/20612917?read-now=1&refreqid=excelsior%3A6d5fdd63eb630a1d7b084a1f0285fa38&seq=7#page_scan_tab_contents

"Dangerous Jobs – Choker Setter." *Black Diamond Now*, 2013, https://www.blackdiamondnow.net/black-diamond-now/2015/04/dangerous-jobs-choker-setter.html

"Decennial Population, City of Seattle: 1900-2000." *City of Seattle Strategic Planning Office*, 12 April 2001, https://www.seattle.gov/Documents/Departments/OPCD/Demographics/DecennialCensus/1900to2000DecennialPopulationOverview.pdf

del Mar, David Peterson. "George Abernethy (1807-1877)." *The Oregon Encyclopedia*, The Oregon Historical Society, 17 March 2018, https://oregonencyclopedia.org/articles/abernethy_george_1807_1877_/#.XvNymEBFyUk

"The Depression of the Mid-1890s." *Digital History*, 2019, http://www.digitalhistory.uh.edu/disp_textbook.cfm?smtID=2&psid=3125

Elmer, Jeffrey L. "Simon Benson." *Oregon Bios Project*, September 2006, http://jtenlen.drizzlehosting.com/ORBios/sbenson.html

Engeman, Richard H. "History of the Oregon Historical Society." *The Oregon Historical Society*, 2020, https://ohs.org/about-us/history.cfm

---. "Town Beginnings." *The Oregon History Project*, The Oregon Historical Society, 2014, https://oregonhistoryproject.org/articles/town-beginnings/#.XtBJTUBFyUk

"Ephraim Shay: American Inventor." *Encyclopaedia Britannica*, 15 April 2020, https://www.britannica.com/science/science

"ESCO Choker Bell." *Van Natta Forestry and Logging with Native Birds, Plants, and Animals*, 20 Dec. 2012, http://www.vannattabros.com/iron39.html

"Greetings from PdxHistory.com." *PdxHistory.com*, 2020, http://www.pdxhistory.com/

Harrybiped. "Abernethy Cemetery." *Harrybipedhiking: The Great Outdoors off the Beaten Path*, 24 Dec. 2018, https://harrybipedhiking.wordpress.com/2018/12/24/abernethy-cemetery/

Haruta, Devanney. "The Rise and Fall of the Marquam Grand: A Tragedy." *All Classical Portland*, 23 June 2016. https://www.allclassical.org/the-rise-and-fall-of-the-marquam-grand-a-tragedy/

"Hiking from Portland to the Pacific Coast." *Oregon Field Guide*, Oregon Public Broadcasting, 8 Aug. 2017, https://www.opb.org/television/programs/ofg/segment/hiking-from-portland-to-the-pacific-coast/

Himes, George H. "History of the Press of Oregon, 1839~1850." *Oregon Historical Quarterly*, Vol. 3, 1902, pp. 327-70, *HathiTrust*, https://babel.hathitrust.org/cgi/pt?id=uva.x030227409&view=1up&seq=359#

"Historic Logging in the Pacific Northwest." *VanNatta Logging History Museum of Northwest Oregon*, 11 Dec. 2012, http://www.vannattabros.com/histlog3.html

"History of Portland, Oregon." *United States History*, 2020,
 https://u-s-history.com/pages/h3903.html

Holbrook, Stewart. "The Life of a 'Bull-Cook': A Day in a 1920s Logging Camp." *Stories, Legends, and Lies of Oregon*, July 1926, https://www.offbeatoregon.com/s1303x-tcm-holbrook-bull-cook.html

---. "Simon Benson: The All-Steam Bunyan." *The Sunday Oregonian*, 12 May 1935, p.1.

---. "Simon Benson, Empire Builder." *Banner Journal*, Black River Falls, Wis. 12 June 1935

Hull, Tom. "'More Deadly than War': High-Lead Steam Logging Unit." *Technology and Culture*, vol. 44, no. 2, Apr. 2003, pp. 355–358. *JSTOR*, www.jstor.org/stable/25148111

Kamholz, Edward. "Donkey Engine." *The Oregon Encyclopedia*, Oregon Historical Society, 17 March 2018, https://oregonencyclopedia.org/articles/donkey_engine/#.XsMVUUBFyUk

Kipling, Rudyard. "Ch. 3: American Salmon." *American Notes*, 1891, *The Literature Network*, http://www.online-literature.com/kipling/american-notes/3/

Klein, Maury. "Financing the Transcontinental Railroad." *AP US History Study Guide*, The Gilder Lehrman Institute of American History, 2019, https://ap.gilderlehrman.org/essays/financing-transcontinental-railroad

"Lewis & Clark's Columbia River – 200 Years Later: Abernethy Creek, Washington." *The Columbia River: A Photographic Journey*, 2020, http://columbiariverimages.com/Regions/Places/abernethy_creek.html

"Lewis & Clark's Columbia River – 200 Years Later: Clatskanie, Oregon." *The Columbia River: A Photographic Journey*, 2020, http://columbiariverimages.com/Regions/Places/clatskanie.html

Lockley, Fred. *History of the Columbia River Valley from The Dalles to the Sea*, Vol. 2, S.J. Clarke, 1928, https://babel.hathitrust.org/cgi/pt?id=mdp.39015021226439;view=1up;seq=7

"Logger Killed by Swinging Tree in Yarding Operation." *The National Institute of Occupational Safety and Health*, Centers for Disease Control and Prevention,

28 June 2006, https://www.cdc.gov/niosh/face/stateface/or/04or052.html

"Logging Railroads: History and Operations." *AmericanRails.com*, 5 December 2021. https://www.american-rails.com/logging.html

Loomis, Pamelia Frances. "Diary," 1870s. Transcript in author's private collection.

Nemec, Bethany. "Early Towns and Cities: From Robin's Nest to Stumptown." *End of the Oregon Trail: Historic Oregon City*, 2 April 2019, https://historicoregoncity.org/2019/04/02/early-towns-and-cities/

"Oregon Symphony History." *Oregon Symphony*, 2020, https://www.orsymphony.org/discover/oregon-symphony-history/

"P. M. Troy's Reminiscences of the Olympia Collegiate Institute." *Early History of Thurston County, Washington: Together with Biographies and Reminiscences of Those Identified with Pioneer Days*, Mrs. Georgiana Blankenship, ed., pp. 296-97, Olympia, 1914, *Google Books*, https://books.google.com/books?id=fnYUAAAAYAAJ&pg=PA296&lpg=PA296&dq=olympia+collegiate+institute+history&source=bl&ots=ar7UOZTBWR&sig=ACfU3U2PKbYv0mPa537qynQOmmooh4Lj3g&hl=en&sa=X&ved=2ahUKEwj7_4nK9c_pAhVOqp4KHUGmAe0Q6AEwD3oECAcQAQ#v=onepage&q=olympia%20collegiate%20institute%20history&f=false

Pentilla, Bryan. "Deep River: The Best 'Logging Show' Anywhere." *Chinook Observer*, 19 Oct. 2009, https://www.chinookobserver.com/life/deep-river-the-best-logging-show-anywhere/article_3463a3a1-28f4-5fb4-9c49-29e9bd840350.html

"Portland, OR." *Export/Import Profile*, Agricultural Marketing Service, U.S. Department of Agriculture, https://www.ams.usda.gov/sites/default/files/media/Port%20Profiles%20Portland%20OR.pdf. Accessed 26 May 2020.

"Portland, Oregon Population History: 1890-2018." *Biggest US Cities*, 17 Jan. 2020, https://www.biggestuscities.com/city/portland-oregon

SIMON BENSON

"Railroad History of Portland, OR." *Pacific Railroad Preservation Assoc.*, 2020, http://www.sps700.org/gallery/essays/portlandrailroadhistory.shtml#top

Schwantes, Carlos A. *The Pacific Northwest: An Interpretive History*. University of Nebraska Press, Rev. ed., 1996. *Google Books*, https://books.google.com/books?id=JImlIbueaXcC&pg=PA202&lpg=PA202&dq=rudyard+kipling+cannery&source=bl&ots=QV3ESIZQgx&sig=ACfU3U3v0DPKS2IfOPX58JLzLu3UugthEQ&hl=en&sa=X&ved=2ahUKEwjK1dnIjdPpAhWFoFsKHVpxAHkQ6AEwAnoECAYQAQ#v=onepage&q=rudyard%20kipling%20cannery&f=false

"Simon Benson House." *Portland State University*, 2020, https://www.pdx.edu/alumni/simon-benson-house

"Simon Benson House: 1803 SW Park Avenue, Portland." *Home and the Heart*, http://homeandheartpdx.weebly.com/simon-benson-house.html. Accessed 26 May 2020.

"Spread of the Flames." *San Francisco Call*, 30 August 1896, *California Digital Newspaper Collection*. https://cdnc.ucr.edu/cgi-bin/cdnc?a=d&d=SFC18960830.2.82.1&e=-------en--20--1--txt-txIN--------1

"Steam Donkey Engines." *Mendocino Coast Model Railroad and Historical Society*, https:mcmrhs.org/logging/equipment/steam-donkey-engines/. Accessed 16 October 2023.

Stumped. "Why Is Portland Nicknamed Stumptown?" *Stumped in Stumptown*, 2020, http://www.stumpedinstumptown.com/2011/03/why-is-portland-named-stumptown/

Taubeneck, John A., and Martin E. Hansen. "Deep River Logging Company and Deep River Timber Company: From Beginning to End." *Highline*, December 2017, 4-7.

Thompson, Richard. "Portland Streetcar System." *The Oregon Encyclopedia*, The Oregon Historical Society, 17 March 2018, https://oregonencyclopedia.org/articles/portland_streetcar_system/#.XtvRnUBFyUk

Thompson, Slason. *Cost Capitalization and Estimated Value of American Railways: An Analysis of Current Fallacies*. 3rd ed. Gunthorp-Warren Publishing,

SIMON BENSON

1908, *Google Books*, https://books.google.com/books?id=TepCAAAAIAAJ&pg=PA86&lpg=PA86&dq=railroad+construction+cost+1890&source=bl&ots=eVAv4W3fm5&sig=ACfU3U3wQhwKR4hQJejMWG9D3xHPxCPmjw&hl=en&sa=X&ved=2ahUKEwiFyvi1mLLpAhVfJzQIHRERBhIQ6AEwDnoECAkQAQ#v=onepage&q=railroad%20construction%20cost%201890&f=false

Toll, William. "Building an Urban Center." *The Oregon History Project*, The Oregon Historical Society, 2014, https://oregonhistoryproject.org/narratives/commerce-climate-and-community-a-history-of-portland-and-its-people/the-mature-distribution-center/building-an-urban-center/#.XtBNvkBFyUk

Unander, Sig. "Building Air Castles: Simon Benson's Lasting Oregon Legacy." *1859: Oregon's Magazine*, 24 April 2018, pp. 82-87, https://1859oregonmagazine.com/think-oregon/history/oregon-history-simon-bensons-legacy/

"Wagon Train." *Encyclopaedia Britannica*, 2020,
>https://www.britannica.com/topic/wagon-train

Whitten, David O. "The Depression of 1893." *EH.net*, Economic History Association, https://eh.net/encyclopedia/the-depression-of-1893/. Accessed 14 May 2020.

"Wigwam Burner." *VanNatta Logging History Museum of Northwest Oregon*, 3 Aug. 2013, http://www.vannattabros.com/histlog26.html

Chapter 4

Allen, Alice Benson. *Simon Benson: Northwest Lumber King*, Binfords and Mort, 1971.

"Almanac: When Japan Attacked Oregon." *CBS News*, 9 Sept. 2018, https://www.cbsnews.com/news/almanac-when-japan-attacked-oregon/

Andrews, Ralph W. *Glory Days of Logging*, Schiffer, 1994.

"Benson Lumber Ceases Operation." *San Diego Tribune*, 7 Sept. 1950.

"The Big Leary Raft." *The New York Times* 9 July 1891, p. 2, https://timesmachine.nytimes.com/timesmachine/1891/07/09/issue.html?action=click&contentCollection=Archives&module=LedeAsset&region=ArchiveBody&pgtype=article.

Binus, Joshua. "Log Rafts, 1902." *The Oregon History Project*, Oregon Historical Society, 2018, https://oregonhistoryproject.org/articles/historical-records/log-rafts-1902/#.Wy3HtfZFx9A.

Casson, Lionel. *Ships and Seamanship in the Ancient World*. Princeton UP, 1995, *Google Books,* https://books.google.com/books?id=sDpMh0gK2OUC&pg=PA4&lpg=PA4&dq=log+rafts+theophrastus&source=bl&ots=SCHY8ahznp&sig=Gr25OqFy8nqviKS2yiVSbvGBTZk&hl=en&sa=X&ved=0ahUKEwj387ny2s_bAhUHJHwKHd1HDE4Q6AEIYDAK#v=onepage&q=log%20rafts%20theophrastus&f=false.

Castagna, Michael. *Shipworms and Other Marine Borers*, Fishery Leaflet 505, United States Department of the Interior, Fish and Wildlife Service, Bureau of Commercial Fisheries, 1961, https://spo.nmfs.noaa.gov/sites/default/files/legacy-pdfs/leaflet505.pdf

"Columbia River Exports Set a New High Record." *The National Lumberman*, 7 April 1922, *Google Books*, https://books.google.com/books?id=FAFOAAAAYAAJ&pg=PA20&lpg=PA20&dq=oj+evenson&source=bl&ots=EUC3mDxKct&sig=gdiv31BQMZVLLtyizpzpsjyBY9I&hl=en&sa=X&ved=0ahUKEwj23OuzgMrbAhXAFTQIHeRAAxkQ6AEITTAI#v=onepage&q=oj%20evenson&f=false.

Crawford, Richard. "The Benson Rafts." *San Diego Yesterday*, 26 Jan. 2008, http://www.sandiegoyesterday.com/wp-content/uploads/2018/12/Benson-Rafts3.pdf .

---. "The Boom of the Eighties." *San Diego Yesterday*, 23 Feb. 2008, http://www.sandiegoyesterday.com/wp-content/uploads/2011/06/boom80s.pdf

"Decennial Population, City of Seattle: 1900-2000." *City of Seattle Strategic Planning Office*, 12 April 2001, https://www.seattle.gov/Documents/Departments/OPCD/Demographics/DecennialCensus/1900to2000DecennialPopulationOverview.pdf.

"Early Statehood: 1850-1880s: The Rise of Los Angeles." *Picture This: California Perspectives on American History*. Oakland Museum of California, http://picturethis.museumca.org/timeline/early-statehood-1850-1880s/rise-los-angeles/info. Accessed 1 February 2022

Elmer, Jeffrey L. "Simon Benson." *Oregon Bios Project*, September 2006, http://jtenlen.drizzlehosting.com/ORBios/sbenson.html

Evenson, O.J. "Speech for Broadcast, 27 May 1962." *San Diego History Center Archives*, San Diego, California.

Evenson, W.T. *Ocean Log Rafts*, unpublished draft, n.d., author's collection.

Fastabend, J. A. "A Brief History of the Oceangoing Raft Business." Personal letter, n.d., author's collection.

"Fire Sweeps Log Raft at Sea; Benson Head Hints Sabotage." *San Diego Union*, 20 September 1940.

Foster, Chris. "A Cheap Shipping Alternative in the Early 1900s, These Benson Log Rafts Are Incredible!"

Dusty Old Thing, 2020,
https://dustyoldthing.com/benson-log-rafts/

Gordon, Greg. "Astoria and Columbia River Railroad." *The Oregon Encyclopedia*, Oregon Historical Society, 2018,
https://oregonencyclopedia.org/articles/astoria_and_columbia_river_railroad/#.Wy1BjvZFx9A

"The Great Lumber Raft." *Sawkill Lumber Co.*, 15 Sept. 2012, https://www.sawkill.nyc/the-great-lumber-raft/

"Historical General Population City and County of Los Angeles, 1850-2010." *Los Angeles Almanac*. Given Place Media, 2018,
http://www.laalmanac.com/population/po02.php.

"History." *Weyerhaeuser*, 2018,
https://www.weyerhaeuser.com/company/history/.

Holbrook, Stewart H. *Holy Old Mackinaw: A Natural History of the American Lumberjack*, Northwest Corner Books, 2016.

---. "Monster of the Sea." *Oakland Tribune*, 18 June 1939, *Newspapers.com*, https://www.newspapers.com/image/136185792/?terms=%22Benson+raft%22.

John, Finn J.D. "First Seaworthy Log Raft Helped Oregon Build San Diego." *Offbeat Oregon*, 19 Feb. 2012, http://www.offbeatoregon.com/1202c-benson-log-rafts-built-city-of-san-diego.html.

Juillerat, Lee. "Balloon Bombs." *Oregon Encyclopedia*, 18 May 2023, https://www.oregonencyclopedia.org/articles/balloon_bombs/

"Lewis & Clark's Columbia River – 200 Years Later: Log Rafts, Washington and Oregon." *The Columbia River: A Photographic Journey*, 2014, http://columbiariverimages.com/Regions/Places/log_rafts.html

"Log Raft." *Historic Hood River*, 2021, http://historichoodriver.com/index.php?showimage=380

MacMullen, Jerry. "Logs from Oregon: History Was in Tow." *The San Diego Union*, 19 Feb. 1961.

Mead, Albert E. "The Log Raft Goes to Sea." *The Manning Times*, 1 February 1922, https://www.newspapers.com/image/?clipping_id=51110398&fcfToken=eyJhbGciOiJIUzI1NiIsInR5cCI6IkpXVCJ9.eyJmcmVlLXZpZXctaWQiOjY4MjQzODY0LCJpYXQiOjE2NDM3O

Miller, Lena Fastabend. "J.A. Fastabend and Pacific Northwest Log Rafts." *Oregon Historical Quarterly*, vol. 6, no. 2 (June 1965), pp. 179-82. *JSTOR*, https://www.jstor.org/stable/20612860?read-now=1&refreqid=excelsior%3Ad6f221c649fb6218643f015a0aa558bc&seq=1#page_scan_tab_contents

"The Miranda. The Joggins Raft. Leary v. The Miranda. New York, N. F. & H. S. S. Co., Limited, V. Leary." *The Federal Reporter*, 26 June 1890, https://law.resource.org/pub/us/case/reporter/F/0043/0043.f.0309.pdf

"O.J. Evenson." *Portrait and Biographical Record: Portland and Vicinity, Oregon*. Chapman, 1903, pp. 660-61, https://archive.org/stream/portraitbiographor00chic#page/660/mode/2up.

"Ocean Timber Rafts." *The American Architect and Building News*, vol. XCII, July-Dec. 1907, *Google Books*, https://books.google.com/books?id=1RILAQAAMAAJ&pg=PA52&lpg=PA52&dq=leary+rafts&source=bl&ots=7l2wBfXmrm&sig=R8OS-EemEMzdYx63644iNqw3xiM&hl=en&sa=X&ved=0ahUKEwic5pyHq9fbAhVpqVQKHdh8CxMQ6AEIPTAD#v=onepage&q=leary%20rafts&f=false.

Olsen, Erik. Engineer for Steam Tug *Hercules*, San Francisco Maritime National Historical Park. Personal interview, 5 Sept., 2018.

"Personal Factors." *The Timberman*, November 1919, *Google Books*, https://books.google.com/books?id=M0c1AQAAMAAJ&pg=PA50&lpg=PA50&dq=benson+raft+the+timberman&source=bl&ots=GDtWW80ErI&sig=FTDKyAxG8MVDzJ_wDtCqf8l0xnY&hl=en&sa=X&ved=0ahUKEwiKnfa-r-vbAhXBlVQKHf5yC7oQ6AEIcDAN#v=onepage&q=benson%20raft%20the%20timberman&f=false.

"Portland, Oregon Population History: 1890-2016." *Biggest U.S. Cities*, 3 Oct. 2017, https://www.biggestuscities.com/city/portland-oregon.

"Railroad History of Portland, OR." *Pacific Railroad Preservation Organization*, 2016, http://www.sps700.org/gallery/essays/portlandrailroadhistory.shtml.

Roach, John. "Seattle Waterfront Falling to Gribble Invasion." *National Geographic News*, 23 April 2004, https://news.nationalgeographic.com/news/2004/04/0423_040423_gribbles.html.

"Seeing the Forest for the Trees: Placing Washington's Forests in Historical Context." *Center for the Study of the Pacific Northwest*, University of Washington, http://www.washington.edu/uwired/outreach/cspn/Website/Classroom%20Materials/Curriculum%20Packets/Evergreen%20State/Section%20II.html. Accessed 12 June 2018.

"Slough." *Dictionary.com*, 2020, https://www.dictionary.com/browse/slough

Smith, Jeff. "Imperial Valley Floods, 1905-'07." *The San Diego Reader* 17 July 2003, https://www.sandiegoreader.com/news/2003/jul/17/imperial-valley-floods-1905-07/#

Sperry, Robert L. "When the Forest Came to San Diego." *Westerners: The Wrangler, San Diego Corral*, March 1976.

Uenuma, Francine. "In 1945 a Japanese Balloon Bomb Killed Six Americans, Five of Them Children, in Oregon." *Smithsonian Magazine*, 22 May 2019, https://www.smithsonianmag.com/history/1945-japanese-balloon-bomb-killed-six-americansfive-them-children-oregon-180972259/

United States Census Bureau. "Number of Inhabitants." *Supplement for California: Population, Agriculture, Manufactures, Mines and Quarries.* 1910, https://www2.census.gov/prod2/decennial/documents/36894832v2ch02.pdf.

"A Water Pipeline from Oregon to California?" *Union-Tribune*, San Diego, Cal., 10 April 2015, https://www.sandiegouniontribune.com/opinion/editorials/sdut-water-pipeline-oregon-california-columbia-2015apr10-story.html.

Woodward, G.H. "Letter to Mr. Lee Passmore, 27 May 1925," *San Diego History Center Archives*, San Diego, California.

Chapter 5

Abbott, Carl. *The Great Extravaganza: Portland and the Lewis and Clark Exposition,* Rev. ed., Oregon Historical Society, 1996.

---. "Lewis and Clark Exposition." *The Oregon Encyclopedia*, Oregon Historical Society, 17 March 2018, https://oregonencyclopedia.org/articles/lewis_clark_exposition/#.W9NWvPZFyUk

---. "Portland (Essay)." *The Oregon Encyclopedia*, Oregon Historical Society, 10 July 2019, https://oregonencyclopedia.org/articles/portland/#.Xs3YZUBFyUk

Allen, Alice Benson. *Simon Benson: Northwest Lumber King.* Binfords and Mort, 1971.

"America's Top Historic Hotels." *Forbes*, Forbes Media LLC, 2 July 2013, https://www.forbes.com/sites/forbestravelguide/2013/07/02/americas-top-historic-hotels/?sh=5cf3824f783b.

Ballestrem, Val. "Albert E. Doyle (1877-1928)." *The Oregon Encyclopedia,* The Oregon Historical Society, Aug. 2018, https://oregonencyclopedia.org/articles/doyle_albert_e/#.W7rHl_ZFyUk

Bean, Alex. "The Blackstone Hotel's Presidential Architecture and History." *Chicago Detours*, 19 Feb. 2018, https://www.chicagodetours.com/blackstone-hotel-history/

Beard, James. *Delights and Prejudices*, Smithmark, 1964.

"Benson Bubblers." *Portland Water Bureau.* The City of Portland, Oregon, 2018, https://www.portlandoregon.gov/water/article/352768

Brandt, Anthony. "Sex, Dog Meat, and the Lash: Odd Facts about Lewis and Clark." *National Geographic*, 8 Dec. 2003, https://www.nationalgeographic.com/news/2003/12/lewis-clark-expedition-history/

Buckley, Jay H. "Lewis and Clark Expedition." *Britannica*, https://www.britannica.com/event/Lewis-and-Clark-Expedition/Pacific-Ocean-and-return. Accessed 12 February 2022.

Crawford, Richard. "The Benson Rafts." *San Diego Yesterday*, 26 Jan. 2008, http://www.sandiegoyesterday.com/wp-content/uploads/2018/12/Benson-Rafts3.pdf

"Decline to Close Down." *The Morning Astorian*, Astoria, Oregon, 6 July 1904, *Newspapers.com*, https://www.newspapers.com/image/351816081/?terms=Benson%2BLumber

"Frederick Taylor and Scientific Management." *Mind Tools*, 2020, https://www.mindtools.com/pages/article/newTMM_Taylor.htm

Gershon, Livia. "How American Tourism Began." *JSTOR Daily*, ITHAKA, 13 June 2016, https://daily.jstor.org/how-tourism-began/

Grundhauser, Eric. "Portland's Love Affair with Its Special Water Fountains." *Atlas Obscura*, 24 March 2017, https://www.atlasobscura.com/articles/portland-benson-bubblers.

"Hey, Entered Yet? No, Well, Do It Now." *The Sunday Oregonian*, 14 May 1916, sec. 1, p. 12, https://oregonnews.uoregon.edu/lccn/sn83045782/1916-05-14/ed-1/seq-12/.

Holbrook, Stewart. *Holy Old Mackinaw*, MacMillan, 1942.

"Hotel History." *The Benson*, The Benson Hotel, 2018, http://bensonhotel.com/portland-hotel/history-of-the-benson-hotel/.

Killen, John. "Past Tense Oregon: Lewis & Clark Exposition Opened 110 Years Ago, Put Portland on the Map." *OregonLive*, The Oregonian, 1 June 2015, https://www.oregonlive.com/history/2015/06/past_tense_oregon_lewis_clark.html.

Larson, Zeb. "Benson Bubblers." *The Oregon Encyclopedia*, 3 February 2021, https://www.oregonencyclopedia.org/articles/benson_bubblers/#.YgIZDIjMK3A.

"Lewis and Clark Centennial Exposition, Forestry Building, Portland, OR." *PCAD*, 2022, https://pcad.lib.washington.edu/building/13170/ .

"Loggers May Form Combination Here." *The Oregon Daily Journal*, Portland, Oregon, 28 June 1904, *Newspapers.com*, https://www.newspapers.com/image/78383355/?terms=Benson%2BLumber

"Northwestern News Notes." *The Post-Intelligencer*, Seattle, Washington, 5 May 1899, p. 11, https://chroniclingamerica.loc.gov/lccn/sn83045604/1899-05-05/ed-1/seq-11/#date1=1899&index=8&rows=20&words=Oak+Point&searchType=basic&sequence=0&state=Washington&date2=1899&proxtext=oak+point&y=12&x=13&dateFilterType=yearRange&page=1

"Oregon News." *The Review*, Roseburg, Oregon, 11 April 1911, *Newspapers.com*, https://www.newspapers.com/image/97559780/

"Portland Hotels." *PdxHistory.com*, 2017, http://www.pdxhistory.com/html/portland_hotels.html

"Portland, United States, 1905: Lewis and Clark Centennial Exposition and Oriental Fair." *America's Best History*, 2017, https://americasbesthistory.com/wfportland1905.html

"Scientific Management." *The Economist*, 9 Feb. 2009, https://www.economist.com/news/2009/02/09/scientific-management

The Simon Benson Story. KOIN-TV, Portland, Oregon. Mid-1960s.

"State News." *The Star*, Seattle, Washington, 22 June 1899, p. 2, https://chroniclingamerica.loc.gov/lccn/sn87093407/1899-06-22/ed-1/seq-2/#date1=1899&index=1&rows=20&words=Benson+s&searchType=basic&sequence=0&state=Washington&date2=1899&proxtext=S.+Benson&y=0&x=0&dateFilterType=yearRange&page=1

Weisensee, Erika. "Portland Rose Festival." *The Oregon Encyclopedia,* Oregon Historical Society, 17 March 2018, https://oregonencyclopedia.org/articles/portland_rose_festival/#.W7QubfZFyUk

Willingham, William F. "Benson Hotel." *The Oregon Encyclopedia*, Oregon Historical Society, 17 March 2018, https://oregonencyclopedia.org/articles/benson_hotel/#.W9P4PPZFyUk

"World's Fair Timeline." *ExpoMuseum*, Urso Chappell, 2015, http://www.expomuseum.com/history/

Chapter 6

Abbott, Carl. *The Great Extravaganza: Portland and the Lewis and Clark Exposition,* rev. ed., Oregon Historical Society, 1996.

Allen, Alice Benson. *Simon Benson: Northwest Lumber King.* Binfords and Mort, 1971.

Burns, Adam. "Railroads in the Gilded Age (1880s)." *American-Rails.com*, 9 December 2021, https://www.american-rails.com/1880s.html.

"CPI Inflation Calculator." *Official Data Foundation*, Alioth LLC, 2019, http://www.in2013dollars.com/1905-dollars-in-2013?amount=8

Duncan, Don. "100 Years Later, Seattle's First World's Fair Remembered." *The Seattle Times Pacific NW Magazine*, 2009,
https://www.seattletimes.com/pacific-nw-magazine/100-years-later-seattles-first-worlds-fair-remembered/

Elswick, Frank. "The Origins of America's Good Roads Movement." *Midwest*, 18 May 2016,
https://blog.midwestind.com/america-good-roads-movement/

"Facts." *Columbia Gorge Info*, n.d.,
http://www.columbiarivergorge.info/facts.html

Fahl, Ronald J. "S.C. Lancaster and the Columbia River Highway: Engineer as Conservationist." *Oregon Historical Quarterly*, vol. 74, no. 2 (June 1973), pp. 101-44, *JSTOR*
https://www.jstor.org/stable/20613352?read-now=1&refreqid=excelsior%3A9b207978f5b76abc502d240366772403&seq=10#page_scan_tab_contents

Friend, E. Michael, and John Hardham. *King of Roads*, Wasco County Historical Museum Press, 2016.

SIMON BENSON

"Good Roads Progress: Simon Benson Declares Portlanders Fail to Realize Significance of the Columbia Highway; Motor Trips to the Inland Empire." *The Oregon Sunday Journal*, 7 June 1914, *Newspapers.com*, https://www.newspapers.com/image/78419412/?terms=simon%2Bbenson%2Bhighway

Gorman, John. "A Portland Lumber Baron's Legacy." *Garden-Fountains.com*, Wayback Machine Internet Archive, archived 17 March 2008, https://web.archive.org/web/20080317100640/http://www.garden-fountains.com/articles/benson-bubblers.html

Halvorson, Gary D. "Oregon Department of Transportation Agency History." *Oregon State Archives*, 2009, https://sos.oregon.gov/archives/records/agency/Documents/transportation-history.pdf

"Henry Lee Bowlby (1879-1948)." *Recreating the Columbia River Highway*, https://sites.google.com/view/recreatingthecrh/people/bowlby-henry-lee. Accessed 15 February 2022.

"Highway and Benson Park Are Dedicated." *Oregon Daily Journal*, 6 September 1915, https://www.newspapers.com/image/77164395/?terms=Multnomah%20Falls%3B%20Benson&match=1.

"History of the Bicycle." *Bicycle History*, 2019, http://www.bicyclehistory.net/bicycle-history/history-of-bicycle/

Hugill, Peter J. "Good Roads and the Automobile in the United States 1880-1929." *Geographical Review*, vol. 72, no. 3 (July 1982), pp. 327-49, *JSTOR*, https://www.researchgate.net/publication/277491527_Good_Roads_and_the_Automobile_in_the_United_States_1880-1929.

Kale, Shelley. "Overview: What Was the PPIE?" *Panama-Pacific International Exposition: 100 Years, 1915-2015*, 2020, https://ppie100.org/history/#article-2.

Kelly, Susan Croce. "Good Roads Movement: United States History." *Encyclopaedia Britannica*, 2015, https://www.britannica.com/event/Good-Roads-movement

The King of Roads. Directed by Daniel Hill, narration by Dan Nims, Crystal Rose Productions, 2016.

Lancaster, Samuel Christopher. *The Columbia: America's Great Highway through the Cascade Mountains to the Sea*. Schiffer Publishing, 2004.

Law, Gary R. *Saving the Crown Jewel of the Columbia Gorge*, Friends of Vista House, 2018.

"A Legend of Multnomah Falls: A Wasco Legend." *First People*, https://www.firstpeople.us/FP-Html-Legends/ALegendOfMultnomahFalls-Wasco.html. Accessed 19 February 2022.

"Lewis and Clark's Columbia River – 200 Years Later: Railroads, Trains and Tracks, etc." *The Columbia River: A Photographic Journey*, Lyn Topinka, 2019, http://columbiariverimages.com/Regions/Places/railroads.html

Lockley, Fred. *History of the Columbia River Valley, from The Dalles to the Sea*, vol. 2. S. J. Clarke, 1928, https://babel.hathitrust.org/cgi/pt?id=mdp.39015021226439;view=1up;seq=7

Marshall, Edward. "Samuel Hill, 'Father of Good Roads,' Tells of the Progress Made in the Enterprise He Originated and of Other Phases of the Good Roads Idea in This Country." *The New York Times*, 17

August 1913, *Newspapers.com*, https://www.newspapers.com/image/20298591/?terms=%22samuel%2Bhill%22

"Maryhill Loops Road." *Maryhill Museum of Art*, 2019, https://www.maryhillmuseum.org/outside/historic-maryhill-loops-road

Mershon, Clarence E. *The Columbia River Highway: From the Sea to the Wheat Fields of Eastern Oregon*, Guardian Peaks Enterprises, 2006.

Miller, Mechelle. "The Legend of Multnomah Falls." *Native American Antiquity*, 31 Jan. 2013, http://nativeamericanantiquity.blogspot.com/2013/01/the-legend-of-multnomah-falls.html

"Mission and History." *The League of American Bicyclists*, 2021, https://www.bikeleague.org/content/mission-and-history.

Multnomah Falls, USDA Forest Service, Columbia Gorge Natural Scenic Area, n.d.

"Multnomah Falls History – the Bridge over the Falls." *Mount Hood History: Mt. Hood and the Gorge's Past*, 23 Nov., 2019, www.mounthoodhistory.com/columbia-river-highway/the-bridge-over-multnomah-falls

Ochi, Diane. *Columbia River Highway: Options for Conservation and Reuse*, 1981, http://npshistory.com/publications/columbia-river-highway.pdf.

"Old Clipping Tells of Benson Cabin; Contributions to Highway." *The Clatskanie Chief*, 13 July 2000: 2. http://ctk.stparchive.com/Archive/CTK/CTK071320 00P02.php?tags=simon|benson.

Parker, Harold. "Good Roads Movement." *The Annals of the American Academy of Political and Social Science*, vol. 40 (March 1912), pp. 51-57, *JSTOR*, https://www.jstor.org/stable/1012795?seq=1#metad ata_info_tab_contents.

Paulus, Michael J., Jr. "Barge Ports on the Columbia and Snake Rivers." *History Link.org*, 8 Dec. 2010, https://www.historylink.org/File/9659

"The Penny Farthing Bicycle." *Pipecraft*, https://www.pipecraft.co.uk/blog/the-penny-farthing-bicycle/. Accessed 28 February 2024.

"Railroad History in Portland, OR." *Pacific Railroad Preservation Association*, 2019, http://www.sps700.org/gallery/essays/portlandrailroadhistory.shtml

"Railroads." *Northwest Power and Conservation Council*, 2019, https://www.nwcouncil.org/reports/columbia-river-history/railroads

Robbins, William G. "Native Cultures and the Coming of Other People: The Lewis and Clark Expedition." *The Oregon History Project*, 2002, https://oregonhistoryproject.org/narratives/this-land-oregon/the-first-peoples/the-lewis-and-clark-expedition/#.XW3DN3dFyUk

Roe, JoAnn. "*Road of Difficulties: Building the Lower Columbia River Highway* by Michael Taylor." *Oregon Historical Quarterly*, vol 109, no. 3 (Fall 2008), pp. 497-98, *JSTOR*, https://www.jstor.org/stable/20615892?read-now=1&refreqid=excelsior%3A0c6374d26ec877e1061a61b635c4281e&seq=2#page_scan_tab_contents.

"Simon Benson (1851-1942)." *Recreating the Columbia River Highway*, https://sites.google.com/view/recreatingthecrh/people/benson-simon. Accessed 15 February 2022.

Tanquist, Jerry, and Ron McCoy. "The Columbia River and Northern Railway." *History: The Pacific Northwest Chapter, National Railway Historical Society*, April 2014, https://www.pnwc-nrhs.org/history_Columbia_River_Northern_Railway.html

"Vista House History." *Columbia River Gorge: Vista House*, 2016. http://www.vistahouse.com/history/

Willis, Peg. *Building the Columbia River Highway: They Said It Couldn't Be Done*, History Press, 2014.

Chapter 7

Allen, Alice Benson. *Simon Benson: Northwest Lumber King.* Binfords and Mort, 1971.

"Arvid Fairbanks Creates Medallion of Benson Service." *The Eugene Daily Guard*, 17 May 1924, *Newspapers.com*, https://www.newspapers.com/image/96911128/?terms=simon%2Bbenson

SIMON BENSON

"Benson Day at Fair Is a Success." *The Daily Oregon Statesman*, 25 Aug. 1915, *Newspapers.com*, https://www.newspapers.com/image/198435700/?terms=simon%2Bbenson%2Bsan%2Bfrancisco

"Benson Polytechnic High School." *Place and See*, 2022, https://placeandsee.com/wiki/benson-polytechnic-high-school.

"Capacity of One Liberty Ship." *United States Merchant Marine*, 2007, http://www.usmm.org/capacity.html.

"Columbia Gorge Hotel, Oregon." *Northwest Travel and Life*, 30 May 2018, https://nwtravelmag.com/columbia-gorge-hotel-oregon/

"Coolidge's 1924 Income Tax Over Double Previous Year." *The Roseburg News-Review*, 1 Sept. 1925, https://www.newspapers.com/image/94031917/?terms=simon%2Bbenson

"Death Summons Oregon Philanthropist." *The Oregonian*, 6 Aug. 1942, *Oregon Pioneer Obituaries*, https://sites.google.com/site/oregonpioneerobituaries/oregon-pioneer-deaths---out-of-state/simon-benson

SIMON BENSON

"Exposition Has Special Day for Oregon's Most Distinguished Citizen: Simon Benson Recipient of High Honor." *The San Francisco Chronicle*, 18 Aug. 1915: 4. *Newspapers.com*, https://www.newspapers.com/image/27362565/?terms=Benson&match=1.

"Facts and History." *Long Beach, California*, https://www.visitlongbeach.com/about-long-beach/facts-history/ Accessed 18 Dec., 2019.

"First Citizen of Oregon Honored." *The San Francisco Chronicle*, 17 August 1915, 1, *Newspapers.com*, https://www.newspapers.com/image/27362100/?terms=Benson&match=1.

"First Citizen of Oregon Is Here: Simon Benson Chosen by His State to Be Honored at the Exposition." *The San Francisco Chronicle*, 16 Aug. 1915: 8. *ProQuest*, https://www.ezproxy.sfpl.org/login?url=https://www.proquest.com/historical-newspapers/first-citizen-oregon-is-here/docview/574381564/se-2?accountid=35117

"Former Oregonian Visits." *The Eugene Guard*, 3 July 1928. *Newspapers.com*, https://www.newspapers.com/image/97162589/?terms=simon%2Bbenson

Friedman, Ralph. *In Search of Western Oregon*, Caxton, 1990.

Gaille, Brandon. "17 Superb Cecil Rhodes Quotes." *Brandon Gaille: Small Business and Marketing Advice*, Aug. 2017, https://brandongaille.com/17-superb-cecil-rhodes-quotes/

"Good Roads." *Building and Engineering News*, 13 Oct. 1915, *Google Books*, https://books.google.com/books?id=hhNGAQAAMAAJ&pg=RA2-PA42&lpg=RA2-PA42&dq=simon+benson+day+panama+pacific&source=bl&ots=e96i6wqhBE&sig=ACfU3U3CO-ByB2-Q4d7MeQYRCT-XTGMeig&hl=en&ppis=_c&sa=X&ved=2ahUKEwjb0KK9wb7mAhUKvZ4KHfi_DoAQ6AEwBHoECAkQAQ#v=onepage&q=simon%20benson%20day%20panama%20pacific&f=false

"Historic Hotel Del Monte." *Dudley Knox Library*, Naval Postgraduate School, n.d. https://library.nps.edu/hotel-del-monte

"Is Voted Oregon's Most Popular Man." *The Capital Journal*, 28 August 1915, *Newspapers.com*, https://www.newspapers.com/image/64481672/?terms=%22simon%2Bbenson%22%2Bdivorce

Jenkins, Frank. "Comments on the Day's News." *The Medford Mail Tribune*, 11 April 1935, *Newspapers.com*, https://www.newspapers.com/image/97035857/?terms=%22simon%2Bbenson%22%2Bdivorce

Kankrud, Johan, *Eventyrett om Husmannsgutten fra Østre Gasusdal som ble Millionµr*, Mariendals Boktrykkeri, 1959.

Karatzas, Basil. "The Indispensable Liberty Ship." *GCaptain*, 6 July 2014, https://gcaptain.com/indispensable-liberty-ship/

Kearney, Kate. "Back to School: A Historic Overview of Benson Polytechnic HS." *Peter Meijer Architect*, 22 Aug. 2016, http://pmapdx.com/blog-pmafindings/2397/back-to-school-a-historic-overview-of-benson-polytechnic-hs

The King of Roads. Directed by Daniel Hill, narration by Dan Nims, Crystal Rose Productions, 2016.

"Liberty Ships Built by the Oregon Shipbuilding Corporation in Portland, Oregon and by Kaiser – Vancouver, Vancouver, Washington for U.S. Maritime Commission 1941-1945." *USMM*, 6 May 2002, http://www.usmm.org/l/oregonvanc.html

Lipsky, William. *San Francisco's Panama-Pacific International Exposition.* Arcadia, 2005.

"List of Liberty Ships (S-Z)." *Wikipedia*, 14 May 2020, https://en.wikipedia.org/wiki/List_of_Liberty_ships_(S–Z)

Lockley, Fred. *History of the Columbia River Valley, from The Dalles to the Sea*, vol. 2. S. J. Clarke, 1928, https://babel.hathitrust.org/cgi/pt?id=mdp.39015021226439;view=1up;seq=7

"Mrs. Harriet King Becomes Wife of Simon Benson." *The Oregon Sunday Journal*, 7 Nov. 1920, *Newspapers.com*, https://www.newspapers.com/image/78429586/?terms=simon%2Bbenson

"Multnomah Falls." *Historic Columbia River Highway: One Hundred Years of the Poem in Stone*, Office of Oregon Secretary of State Bev Clarno, n.d., https://sos.oregon.gov/archives/exhibits/columbia-river-highway/Pages/history-multnomah-falls.aspx Accessed 18 December. 2019

Murphy, Peter. "A Road Trip through Oregon's Fruit Loop." *1859: Oregon's Magazine*, Nov. 2014, https://1859oregonmagazine.com/explore-oregon/recreation/road-reconsidered-highway-35/

"New Columbia Gorge Hotel Is Open to Public." *The Oregon Daily Journal*, 19 June 1921, *Newspapers.com*, https://www.newspapers.com/image/78429059/?terms=simon%2Bbenson

Panama-Pacific International Exposition, 1915: The World Meets in San Francisco. National Park Service, June 2015.

"Panama-Pacific International Exposition (PPIE), Oregon State Building, San Francisco, CA." *Pacific Coast Architecture Database*, 2020, http://pcad.lib.washington.edu/building/5835/

"Part 4 – Why the Loggers Organized." *Industrial Workers of the World*, https://archive.iww.org/history/library/Chaplin/centralia-conspiracy/4/. Accessed 21 February 2022.

Pinkson, Leon J. "Oregonians to Honor Father of Good Roads in North: Builder of Columbia Highway to Be Feted." *The San Francisco Chronicle*, 15 Aug. 1915: 43. *ProQuest*, https://www.newspapers.com/image/27360971/?terms=Benson&match=1.

Polk's Portland (Oregon) City Directory: 1933, vol. lxviii, Polk and Co., 1933, *Ancestry.com U.S. City Directories, 1922-1995*, https://www.ancestry.com/imageviewer/collections/2469/images/15447590?pId=991643683&backurl=https%3A%2F%2Fwww.ancestry.com%2Ffamily-tree%2Fperson%2Ftree%2F150985847%2Fperson%2F172003763197%2Fstory

Read, Richard. "Columbia Gorge Hotel Finally Lands Buyer with NW Hotelier." *The Oregonian/Oregon Live*, updated 20 Jan. 2019, https://www.oregonlive.com/business/2009/10/columbia_gorge_hotel_finally_l.html

"A Roadside Failure." *The Eugene Register*, 18 Feb. 1930, *Newspapers.com*, https://www.newspapers.com/image/111228982/?terms=simon%2Bbenson

"San Francisco, United States 1915: Panama Pacific International Exposition." *United States World's Fairs*, America's Best History, 2019, https://americasbesthistory.com/usworldsfairs.html

"Simon Benson Dies, Aged 91." *The Statesman-Journal*, 6 Aug. 1942, *Newspapers.com*, https://www.newspapers.com/clip/23242146/simon_benson_18511942/

"Simon Benson, Pioneer Oregon Lumberman, Dies." *The Roseburg News-Review*, 5 August 1942, *Newspapers.com*, https://www.newspapers.com/image/93068757/?terms=simon%2Bbenson%2Bdies

"Simon Benson to Wed Mrs. King of Hood River." *The Oregon Daily Journal*, 3 Nov. 1920, *Newspapers.com*, https://www.newspapers.com/image/78429429/?terms=simon%2Bbenson

Voss, Don, and Grace Voss. *Footsteps to America*. Self-published family history. Accessed 21 February 2022.

Afterword

Connelly, Joel. "The President in a Wheelchair Who Created Our Olympic National Park." *SeattlePI.com*, 29 March 2016. https://www.seattlepi.com/local/politics/article/A-President-in-a-wheelchair-created-Olympic-7213930.php

www.ingramcontent.com/pod-product-compliance
Lightning Source LLC
Chambersburg PA
CBHW062005180426
43198CB00037B/2413